Contents

Preface

Most people setting up in business naturally choose one in which they have already been successful. However, they find that as the owner of a small business, they cannot survive by doing 'what they are good at' all day long. They are soon faced with tasks and responsibilities of which they have no experience – such as selling, or keeping accounts. An important aspect of running a business, for which few people are prepared, is employing staff.

Indeed, some business people are so deterred by the prospect of becoming an employer that they keep their business to a level they can handle personally. In this case the full potential of the business may never be realised.

You may be at the stage yourself where you are considering whether to take on staff, and want to weigh up the pros and cons before taking the plunge. You want to know what plans should be made, how to recruit, what your legal responsibilities will be, and how to avoid problems with your employees. There may be many other questions you wish to ask.

Alternatively you may already employ staff and find that there are some areas where you need specific help.

If you fall into either of these categories this book will help you. It will take you gently through the minefield of employing people, point out some of the pitfalls and show you how you can overcome them. It will demonstrate how succeeding as an employer can really help you succeed in your business.

You will save money by knowing how to choose the right staff and you will see how investment in training can pay dividends. Many of the costly legal battles between employers and employees can be avoided by good employment practices; these practices are explained, in straightforward language.

Being a successful employer is fundamental to the success of a business. It is not always easy – human nature, and the law, are complex. This book has been written to help you on the way.

HOW TO EMPLOY & MANAGE STAFF

In this Series

other titles in preparation

EMPLOY &
MANAGE STAFF

Wendy Wyatt

Northcote House

Acknowledgements

Grateful thanks to my long suffering husband Les, my family and friends, for
their encouragement and forbearance.

British Library Cataloguing in Publication Data
Wyatt, Wendy, 1955-
    How to – employ & manage staff. – (How to).
    1. Business firms. Personnel management
    I. Title
    658.3

    ISBN 0-7463-0554-0

First published in 1989 by Northcote House Publishers Ltd. Harper & Row
House, Estover Road, Plymouth PL6 7PZ. United Kingdom.
Tel: Plymouth (0752) 705251. Fax: (0752) 777603. Telex: 45635.

Typeset by Peregrine Typesetting, Perrancoombe, Perranporth, Cornwall.
Printed in Great Britain by BPCC Wheatons Ltd, Exeter

1
Being an Employer

FIRST THINGS FIRST

What does it actually mean to be an employer?

In hard business terms, an employer can be defined as one who uses other people's labour to expand a business and increase profits. Becoming an employer is clearly a step to consider once your business has grown as far as it can under your own steam.

Of course there are other factors, too. You have an important responsibility to your employees in return for their labour – and these days this extends far beyond the mere payment of wages. You must consider their health, safety and comfort at work and comply with the law which give employees certain rights. You also have a duty towards the state in the deduction of income taxes and national insurance (NI) and in complying with numerous laws and regulations concerning employment.

In addition, there will be paperwork to handle, including personnel records and wages administration. You will, inevitably, have occasional 'problem' staff with whom you will have confrontations, and in some cases even a dismissal could be necessary.

Your staff may well be your biggest expense. Not only will you have to pay salaries but expenses such as employer's NI contributions, holiday pay and sick pay. Accommodation, facilities and equipment for your staff will all cost money, too.

If these can be said to be the problems of employing staff, here are just some of the benefits – and most businesses find that the benefits far outweigh any disadvantages!

- Your business will be able to **expand** in a way it never could if you were running it on your own.

- Employees will bring new and profitable **ideas** into your business.

- By delegating routine work you will be able to **concentrate** on the most profitable areas of your business.

- You will have **more time** to spend with your family as you will no longer have the entire workload of the business on your shoulders.

- As a self-employed person you will no longer feel so **isolated**.

Before considering the various obligations of an employer, it is worth mentioning that the government has given some recognition to the problems faced by employers of small numbers of staff. This has resulted in some exemptions and financial help, including the following:

- **Maternity**. Most pregnant women with over two years' service have the right to return to their jobs after maternity leave. However, in small companies, with five or fewer employees, it is recognised that it could be impractical to keep a job open. In this case the employee cannot claim unfair dismissal.

- **Redundancy Rebates**. Currently, employers with fewer than ten employees may claim a rebate of 35% of the statutory redundancy payment. This facility is, however, likely to be withdrawn when the new Employment Bill becomes law.

- **Disciplinary procedures**. The new Employment Bill includes plans to exempt employers with fewer than 20 employees from providing a note on disciplinary and grievance procedures in the statement of main terms and conditions of service. This bill is likely to become law during 1989.

Employer's Liability Insurance

As an employer, you will have a **statutory duty** to take out Employer's Liability Insurance. This will cover you for personal injuries or diseases suffered by your employees during the course of, or arising because of, their employment with you.

This insurance must be taken out with an **authorised** insurer and the certificate issued must be **displayed** at the place of work, where all employees can see it.

Your insurance broker will be able to advise you on how to obtain Employer's Liability Insurance – and how much it will cost you.

Health and safety at work

Clearly, preventing accidents is far better than claiming against your insurance – from everyone's point of view. So another aspect of becoming an employer which also needs careful consideration is the safety of your staff whilst at work.

Your legal obligation as an employer is to ensure 'as far as reasonably practicable' the health, safety and welfare of those in your employment, during the course of their work. This covers all aspects of providing a safe working environment and working practices, for instance providing well maintained machinery and equipment. Your obligation also extends to the safe handling, storing and transportation of articles and substances. The place of work must be maintained to a high degree of safety with sufficient entrances and exits. You also must provide your staff with information, training and supervision to ensure health and safety at work.

See Appendix One for details of the legal requirements. Provisions regarding accidents, first-aid and fire precautions are covered there, too.

Hours of work

Although there are no general regulations about hours of work, there are some **statutory regulations** which cover certain types of work (see below). Hours of work can also be regulated by trade union agreements or, more likely for small businesses, by the terms of employment which you determine.

When deciding the hours of work don't forget that you will be competing with other local employers for the 'best staff'. 37½ to 40 hours a week are usual for full time jobs – more if you are prepared to pay overtime! If you want your staff to work unsocial hours a **shift premium** is usually paid.

There are no rules regarding office worker's hours but there are restrictions in the hours you can ask your staff to work in the following areas:

Shops   There are rules regarding early closing. The length of time which may be worked without a break and the length of the breaks are defined. There are further regulations regarding the employment of 16 to 18 year olds. (These and other rules are set out in the Shops Acts 1950-65.)

Factories   There are strict rules concerning the hours which may be worked by employees under 18, as outlined in the Factories Act (1961). But there are, in general, no statutory limitations regarding the working hours of adults.

Drivers   Drivers of goods vehicles exceeding 3.5 tonnes gvw work to strict regulations regarding their hours of driving. Records must be kept. See EC regulations 3820/85, 3821/85 and The Driver's Hours (Goods Vehicles) (Keeping of Records) Regulations 1987.

Young people   These are defined by law as being between 16 and 18 years old. In several work situations, other than those mentioned above, there are regulations limiting their hours of work. For details see the Children and Young Persons Act 1933-1969.

If any of the above Acts or regulations apply to your business the relevant information can be purchased from HMSO (Her Majesty's Stationery Office), 49 High Holborn, London WC1V 6HB (01 622 3316) or ordered through booksellers.

Legislation is currently planned to remove the restrictions on young person's hours of work – including night work. Look out for further developments.

Accommodation

It is important to ensure that you have sufficient and comfortable accommodation for your staff – not only to stay in line with current law but to keep your employees content. Bad accommodation can lead to low output, poor quality, and a high turnover in staff.

Offices, shops and factories all have regulations which define acceptable standards of accommodation. These cover overcrowding, sanitary provisions, lighting, temperature, ventilation and seating. They are set out in the Offices, Shops and Railway Premises Act 1963 and the Factories Act.

WHAT RULES SHOULD YOU MAKE?

To run a safe and efficient company inevitably means a certain number of rules. If these are kept to a minimum, well known, and reasonable, they are likely to be respected. Employees want to know where they stand. Far from finding them restrictive they will probably find them helpful.

Once you have been an employer a short while (so you can see which rules are needed) it is a good idea to set them down in writing, giving each employee a copy for reference.

The rules you make will, of course, be determined by the type of business you run, but these are some headings to consider:

Health and safety	Use of company vehicles
Smoking	Private telephone calls
Alcohol	Car parking
Food and drink	What constitutes misconduct
Absence	Gross misconduct
Timekeeping	Disciplinary procedures
Work standards	The grievance procedure

TALKING TO ONE ANOTHER

In all types of company, large and small, lack of communication can be a major problem. It is not one which is always easy to address. Employees find that they are not even given the information they need to do their job properly. 'But I wasn't told!' is a common cry.

Many employees only get a chance to discuss their individual performance once a year at appraisal time. This really isn't adequate – do try to give each person a real chance to talk to you regularly.

If you can find a way of communicating well with your employees, you will have the makings of a good relationship with them. A weekly group briefing and debriefing session works well for many managers – as long as information flows freely in *both* directions! Make sure that your employees know how the business is going and appreciate any problems. These meetings will increase trust between the employer and the employee and should help to avoid misunderstandings.

UNIONS AND YOUR EMPLOYEES

In most small businesses few staff belong to a trades union. However, if several employees decide to join a union they may ask you to recognise it.

There is no statutory obligation to recognize a union. In making your decision you must weigh up the advantages and disadvantages according to your situation. You may decide just to grant **representation rights**. In this case the union may represent individuals in presenting grievances and in disciplinary action. They do not, in this case, have rights to negotiate terms and conditions of employment for your employees. If there is enough employee support for the union, full recognition may follow, provided you consent.

WHO DO YOU NEED TO EMPLOY?

Decisions on what kind of staff to employ, and how many, must not be made in haste. Your goal will be to have the right people, in the right numbers, doing the right job, at the right time. There are, however, many factors which sometimes make this difficult if not impossible!

Planning your workforce carefully is as essential to your business as, say, controlling your cash flow and scheduling the purchase of raw materials. Too often employing a new member of staff is a reaction to a crisis rather than part of a planned development programme. Even if it is a case of replacing a member of staff, the opportunity should be taken to reassess the situation.

Employing the right number of people is a key factor in the success of your business. If you employ too few you may find yourself unable to fulfil orders – a business nightmare! Too few staff may also mean that those you do employ are working under a lot of pressure. This will ultimately mean a high turnover of staff which can make your business unstable.

On the other hand, employing too many staff can be equally disastrous! Firstly it will give you enormous unnecessary expense in wages payments. Secondly it will demoralize your staff – boredom is a major reason why people leave jobs.

Employing too soon or too late will cause similar problems.

In planning your workforce do take note of relevant and up to date information, combined with your past experience. A good start would be to make staffing plans in conjunction with your sales forecasts. You might for example consider:

- market fluctuations
- past employment problems (if appropriate) eg numbers of leavers, past shortages of staff
- seasonal variations in work load
- the extent to which your business is labour intensive
- the numbers of staff you can afford to employ
- the numbers you can accommodate

Remember that problems with seasonal variations and market fluctuations can often be handled economically by the use of **temporary labour**, employed directly by you or through an agency.

External influences, too, will affect your plans and must be considered realistically. These influences can include:

- the local supply of skills

- competition for labour
- the local level of unemployment
- local rates of pay
- transport facilities

You will need to define as precisely as possible:

- what work needs to be done?
- when?
- how much of your work can you delegate?
- what calibre of staff do you need?
- the extent to which you are prepared to train?
- how many people you need?
- whether they will all be doing the same job?
- if not, how you are going to divide the work?

QUESTIONS AND ANSWERS

I have been told that I might be able to take on a school leaver trainee on the YTS scheme. What is YTS? How can I get a trainee? What will it cost me?

YTS is the **Youth Training Scheme**. The scheme offers school leavers work-based training and 20 weeks' college-based training over a two year period. Those starting the scheme at 17 are on YTS for just one year. The standards of the training have been agreed nationally.

The scheme is run by the Training Agency through **Managing Agents** who are approved training organizations. To find out which local Managing Agent is most likely to be able to help you, contact the Training Agency, which is part of the Department of Employment.

Care will be taken by Managing Agents to establish exactly what you will be able to offer a trainee. They will send trainees along for interviews and you will not have to appoint anyone you do not believe will suit you. It is best to take on a trainee at Easter or in the summer months as you will have the pick of the school leavers.

While on the scheme, trainees receive a small allowance. The amount changes annually but, to give you an idea of the amounts involved, the 1988 figure was £29.50 for the first year and £35.00 per week during the second. If the trainee was on a one year course the allowance was £29.50 for the first 13 weeks and £35.00 for the remainder. The employer's contribution to the allowance was in the region of £15.00 per week. Trainees do not have to pay tax or national insurance.

The amount of money trainees receive has attracted cries of

'slave labour' and doubtless a small minority of employers do abuse the system. However, if you can give a trainee real work experience (not filing and photocopying all day!) you may greatly increase the trainee's chances of getting a good job. Many employers decide to keep the result of their training efforts and offer YTS trainees permanent positions in their company.

What is Employment Training?

It is a new national scheme.

At the time of writing, this scheme is in its early days and not without its problems. It was introduced in September 1988. Trainees on the scheme receive unemployment benefit enhanced by £10.00 per week. The cost to employers is £25.00 per week. No tax or national insurance deductions are to be made. Again there are accusations of 'slave labour'.

The philosophy behind the scheme is the same as for the Youth Training Scheme: training will increase the chances of getting a job.

It is also hoped that the scheme will combat future shortages of school leavers. Employers will need to train older people to do the jobs traditionally filled by school leavers.

In this scheme there are new intakes of trainees throughout the year, so there will be no 'best time' to appoint. Trainees receive a week of general training before going to an employer. You should interview trainees before they join you and you can dismiss them if they are unsatisfactory. The training period will last between 3 months and a year, to suit you.

A wide variety of jobs can be undertaken by trainees – the main criterion being that it does in fact include training.

Contact the Training Agency for more details.

I would like to employ disabled people. What help and advice is available?

The **Disablement Advisory Service** is available to help you on all aspects of employing disabled people. They have 71 local offices and can be contacted via your local Jobcentre.

They will advise you of several schemes available to help you – for instance the **Aids to Employment Scheme** where equipment is loaned to help disabled people work. There are also **grants** available if, for example, you need to adapt the premises for disabled workers.

The Disablement Advisory Service also produces leaflets and a Code of Good Practice in employing disabled people.

2
The Recruitment Drive

The importance of appointing the right person for the job cannot be overestimated. If you choose the right people most aspects of running your business will become easier. Errors made at this stage can prove very costly and time-consuming in the future.

You need people whom you can trust to do a good job, quickly and efficiently; people with a steady background and in good health; employees who will be honest and pleasant to work with.

Identifying such paragons is not easy and of course mistakes can sometimes be made. But several problems can be avoided if you spend time working out some good recruitment practices.

MISTAKES TO AVOID

There are also some mistakes you must *not* make – by law!

As soon as you start to think about employing staff you are under a legal obligation not to **discriminate** between race, sex or marital status. Some employers have tried to get around these laws by various means – such as excluding ethnic applicants by demanding a higher standard of spoken or written English than is required to do the job well. These attempts are clearly discriminatory and must be avoided.

Applicants who feel that they have been discriminated against may take their case to an **Industrial Tribunal**. So care must be taken at all stages of the recruitment process.

- Check that your advertisements are not written in a way that may be considered discriminatory, eg by the use of 'he' throughout, expressions such as 'Girl Friday', 'English Rose' and other variations.

- When it comes to the interview it is helpful to use the same format for each interview – for instance, by using your employee specification as the framework. Be careful to ask all applicants broadly the same questions.

- When interviewing female applicants do not fall into the trap of asking questions such as – 'When are you going to get married?' 'When are you going to have children?' or 'What arrangements have you made for child care while you are at work?' You probably won't ask male applicants these questions.

- Applicants belonging to an ethnic minority are often disadvantaged in interviews. They sometimes do not understand the subtleties of the interview, which you may take for granted – such as seeing why an interviewer has put a question a particular way. Always bear in mind that an applicant's ability to handle an interview is not necessarily a reflection on how well he, or she, will do in the job.

Codes of practice explaining in detail how to avoid discrimination in employment are available from the **Commission for Racial Equality** and the **Equal Opportunities Commission**.

Commission for Racial Equality   Equal Opportunities Commission
Elliot House   Overseas House
10/12 Allington Street   Quay Street
London SW1E 5EH   Manchester M3 3HN
01 828 7022   061 833 9244

Applicants other than British or EEC nationals must obtain a **work permit** before employment.

HOW TO ATTRACT APPLICANTS

This stage is crucial. If you fail to attract the right applicants for the job in the first place you cannot possibly hope to appoint the right person for the job!

Not all methods of attracting staff are expensive – if fact many are free! A very efficient way is to ask friends or current employees whether they know anyone who may be interested in applying. However, this *could* lead to discrimination if it reduces the opportunity for both sexes and all races to apply.

Another free source of applicants is the local **Jobcentre**. All you have to do is ring through with details of the vacancy. You can either ask them to telephone you when someone is interested, or ask them to forward application forms. The latter is recommended as Jobcentres do not pre-select and you could waste a lot of time interviewing unsuitable applicants.

Other ways of attracting applicants can be expensive, but are at times necessary, for instance **advertising** your vacancies and using **recruitment agencies**. However, first of all you could give some thought to designing an application form.

The application form

A good application form is well worth the trouble of producing. Its initial use is to help you select applicants for interview. Then it acts as a basis for the interview itself. Later on the successful candidate's application form becomes the cornerstone of your personnel records.

Application forms of unsuccessful, but promising, candidates can form a bank of potential employees to contact next time a vacancy occurs. This practice can save a great deal of time and money.

For executive staff, asking for a CV is probably more appropriate than asking them to complete an application form. CV stands for **curriculum vitae** – Latin for 'course of life'. It is a summary of the applicant's qualifications, experience and achievements. The CV will tell you a great deal about how the applicant sees his or her career. You will also be able to see how well applicants express themselves on paper.

However, in most other cases an application form is a more efficient selection tool as you have a basis for comparing all the candidates. Another great advantage is that you can design it to find out what *you* want to know, rather than being told what the applicant wants you to know!

Here is an example of a very basic application form. You may well need different versions for different levels of staff. For instance a labourer may feel intimidated by a form which emphasises qualifications. There may be several additional questions you will want to add to make the form relevant to your business - for instance specific questions regarding technical knowledge or ability to speak a foreign language. It can be a good idea to allow some space where applicants for a more senior position can say why they should be given the job and the special qualities and skills they could bring to it.

Application Form

Please return the completed Application Form to:

_____

_____

Application for the position of _____

1. Full name _____
   Address _____
   Telephone number _____ Date of birth _____

2. When would you be available to start work? (State notice period
   if appropriate). _____

3. Do you know anyone employed by this Company? If so, whom?

   _____

4. Are you a car driver? _____ Clean licence? _____

5. Please give details of any major operations or medical problems
   you have had in the last five years. _____

   _____

   What is your height? _____ Weight? _____
   Are you willing to have a medical examination? _____
   Are you registered disabled? _____
   If so, please give details of the disability. _____
   What is your RDP number? _____

6. Please give details of your education from the age of 12.
   School/College/University Dates   Qualifications
   _____ _____ _____
   _____ _____ _____
   _____ _____ _____

7. Please give details of major courses attended during your career.
   Course title   Length of course   Year attended
   _____ _____ _____
   _____ _____ _____

8. What are your hobbies and interests? _____

   _____

9. Please give full details of your last three jobs, starting with the most recent.

Company _____ Position held_____

Type of business_____

Address _____ Dates employed

_____ From _____ Until _____

Salary upon leaving/present salary £ _____

Reason for leaving/wishing to leave _____

Describe what the job involved and any particular achievements.

_____

_____

Company _____ Position held_____

Type of business_____

Address_____ Dates employed_____

_____ From _____ Until _____

Salary upon leaving/present salary £ _____

Reason for leaving/wishing to leave _____

Describe what the job involved and any particular achievements.

_____

_____

Company _____ Position held_____

Type of business_____

Address _____ Dates employed_____

_____ From _____ Until _____

Salary upon leaving/present salary £ _____

Reason for leaving/wishing to leave_____

Describe what the job involved and any particular achievements.

_____

_____

10 List any positions held prior to those listed above.

From	Until	Company	Job title
____	____	_____	_____
____	____	_____	_____
____	____	_____	_____
____	____	_____	_____
____	____	_____	_____

11 Give details of two referees. Both should be from previous employers. They will only be contacted after a job offer has been made to you unless we obtain your express permission.

Name	Company/address	Business relationship

12 I confirm that the information I have given on this form is true and complete to the best of my knowledge. I understand that if the information is subsequently found to be false, my application may be rejected, or in the case of my appointment I may be dismissed.

Signature _____ Date _____

Advertising

You may find that you have to advertise your vacancy.

A local paper will be the best medium unless it is a very specialized job you wish to fill. In this case you will be more likely to succeed if you advertise in a national paper or a professional journal.

The advertisement you write needs to do four things. It must:

- seek out suitable applicants;
- tell them about the job;
- make them want to apply;
- tell them how to apply.

The key to success is to see your advertisement through the eyes of the person you want to appoint to the job. Don't be misled into thinking that the success of your advertisement is measured by the quantity of replies you receive – it will succeed if the right *quality* of applicant replies. The ideal advertisement would bring just one perfect applicant through your door half an hour after it appeared!

Stick to a simple format when writing your advertisement:-

- Heading – job title
- Sub-heading – salary. Always give an indication of what you will be paying. Would you apply for a job which didn't?
- Describe the job. Remember to pick out aspects which will interest applicants most – but be careful not to misrepresent the job in any way.
- Describe the successful candidate – in terms of qualifications and experience – thus deterring unsuitable applicants.

- Tell them how to reply – avoid box numbers as these make applicants very suspicious. Put yourself in the position of the applicant – would you respond not knowing who is to see your personal details?
- When asking applicants to reply you can ask them to ring for an application form or to arrange an interview. Alternatively you can request a CV.

Write your advertisement in plain English – stuffily worded advertisements are as offputting as the gimmicky ones! Write short paragraphs of shortish sentences. Check spelling and meaning carefully – for instance, if you run a successful contracting company don't describe it as an 'expanding contracting company'! A national building products company once advertised for 'A Concrete Representative'.

Here is an advertisement which follows the basic rules:

CLERK TYPIST
£6,000 pa

To work in a lively new company selling stationery to businesses. The Clerk Typist will carry out general duties in a hectic office. There will be quite a lot of telephone work – mainly taking stationery orders from customers. A wide variety of typing will be required, including purchase orders and all the principal's correspondence.

The successful applicant will have had at least one year's experience working in an office and will have an RSA II typing qualification as a minimum and preferably 'O' level English.

Please telephone for an application form.
Mr. J. Biggs, Biggs Stationers
01-234-5678

QUESTIONS AND ANSWERS

Some employers use advertising agencies to place their recruitment advertisements. What do the agents do?

One of the most valuable services an advertising agent provides is advice on which media to use – so it is important to use a local agency – unless the vacancy is one you are planning to advertise nationally.

An agent will help you to write and design your advertisement and may be able to negotiate discounts for you.

However if you are only placing a few local advertisements each year, it is unlikely that you will need their services.

Should I monitor the response I get to an advertisement?

Yes. If you don't you will never know if you are wasting money. A record will, over a period of time, establish quite clearly which advertising medium works best for your type of vacancy.

You could keep records with these headings:

Job / Date / Medium / Cost / No. of Replies / No. of Interviews / Offers / Starters.

Recruitment agencies

Recruitment agencies are particularly useful in supplying temporary staff during times of crisis, or during seasonal influxes of work. However to employ permanent staff through an agency is very expensive; **fees** are set at around 15% of the annual salary for office staff. An executive appointment could cost you around 17-20% of the annual salary.

If the people you want to attract are scarce or highly specialized, you may well find agencies' services very good value – especially as there is usually nothing to pay unless you appoint one of their candidates. But do check this before giving them the assignment!

So what do they do for their fees?

Most agencies keep a **register** of people who have approached them looking for work. They will go through the register and select those most likely to suit your requirements. They will then act as 'middleman' between you and the applicants – sorting out interviews, reporting mutual reactions and negotiating job offers. The effectiveness of the agency therefore hinges on the quality of people who have approached them, the agency's ability to select, and your having given them sufficient information to do the job properly!

If you use an agency you will, of course, still have to go through the process of interviewing – but you will only have to see a few pre-selected candidates.

Whichever method of attracting applicants you choose it should fulfil three criteria:

- it must be suitable for the job you are trying to fill;
- it must be within your budget;
- it must be available when you need it.

Crisis!

A problem of nightmare proportions arises when you have done all the 'right things' but have not managed to attract any applicants – or none of the applicants are of the right calibre!

All you can do is review the situation by asking yourself (and answering honestly!) questions such as:-

- Is the salary I am offering too low – for the job? For the locality?
- Am I frightening applicants off by asking too much of them?
- Is the job attractive? Can I make it more so?
- Is the job such an unusual combination of tasks that one person is unlikely to have had the experience I am asking?
- Am I prepared to offer training? (This is often very attractive to applicants.)
- Is my advertisement clear and interesting? Would I apply? Why? Why not?
- Have I chosen the right advertising medium? Would the ideal candidate see it?
- Is it a bad time of year for recruitment? (Just before Christmas and the summer holiday period are the worst.)

SELECTING INTERVIEWEES

So now, all being well, you have a pile of application forms on your desk and the time has come to decide who to interview. Using your employee specification as the guideline, divide applications into three piles:

- probables
- possibles
- rejections

Probables

Don't try to see more than about five people, or you become confused! Try to arrange for all the interviews to take place within a day or two; otherwise you will not remember the applicants clearly and your decision will be less objective.

Decide how long you will need for the interview. An hour is

Invitation to interview

Dear Mrs. White,

Thank you for your recent application for the position of Machine Operator.

We are very interested in your application and would like you to attend an interview on Friday, 4th August at 10.30 am. I should be grateful if you would confirm that you are able to attend.

I enclose a map showing the location of our offices.

Yours sincerely, etc.

Delaying letter

Dear Mr. Thomas,

Thank you for your recent letter regarding the position of Machine Operator.

I am afraid that there will be some delay in letting you know the outcome of your application.

I shall write to let you know whether you will be invited for interview, within the next three weeks.

Yours sincerely, etc.

Rejection letter

Dear Miss Brown,

Thank you for your recent application for the position of Machine Operator. I regret to inform you that, in this instance, it has been unsuccessful.

I would, however, like to thank you for the interest you have shown in our company and I wish you luck in your search for a new position.

Yours sincerely, etc.

usually quite long enough for all but the most senior appointments. Allow additional time if you want the interviewees to carry out a test of some sort. Leave time for yourself, too, at the end of the interview to complete your notes and clear your head. If you do it properly interviewing is a very tiring job! Set aside an hour and a half per person to do the job comfortably.

Set up the interviews as soon as possible. Where practical arrange interviews by telephone to avoid delay. Ring interviewees at work only if you know you can be very discreet. Their current position must not be jeopardized in any way. It is probably best to telephone applicants at home, in the evening.

If for some reason you cannot contact them by 'phone, drop them a line.

If applicants have far to travel you may wish to offer travelling expenses and you could mention this in the letter.

Possibles

Keep on hold just in case the 'probables' are not as good as they appear on paper. If you are going to keep possibles waiting for more than a fortnight send them a delaying letter.

If you later decide not to see these people don't forget to send a standard rejection letter (see below).

Rejections

It is courteous to send a letter without delay. Here is an example.

In all your dealings with applicants – those you see and those you reject at an early stage – never forget that all you do will be good, or bad, public relations for your business. Applicants who never receive an acknowledgment of their application won't hesitate to be critical of your business. On the other hand some rejection letters can be so kind that applicants are almost pleased to receive them!

CHECKLIST

Attracting applicants

- How are you planning to attract applicants for the job?

- Why do you think your approach most likely to work?

- How much will it cost to complete?

Advertising

- Are you sure you've chosen the best medium?
- Will suitable applicants want to apply?
- Will unsuitable applicants realise that the job is not for them?
- Have you told applicants how to reply?
- Sure that your advertisement does not discriminate unlawfully?

3
The Job Interview

Interviews can sometimes be as nerve-racking for the interviewer as they are for the interviewee, especially if you are inexperienced! Careful preparation for each candidate is the key to successful and confident interviews.

PLANNING THE INTERVIEW

Always re-read the applicant's details immediately before the interview. You should have already prepared a list of questions linked to your job specification. These will help you treat each applicant the same and ensure that you don't forget to ask anything. Also, each completed application form will raise further questions in your mind; it is a good idea to make a note of these before the interview. Further questions will arise naturally, prompted by what the candidate says during the interview.

Make sure that your interview follows a logical sequence, otherwise it can become an aimless chat which leaves you none the wiser about the applicant's abilities. This structure works well:

- Phase One   Setting the scene.
- Phase Two   Assessing the applicant.
- Phase Three   Telling the applicant about the job.
- Phase Four   Telling the applicant when to expect the result.

Setting the scene
This starts before the applicant arrives. Firstly, are you going to conduct interviews over a desk (especially cleared for the event!), or

more informally, for instance in comfortable chairs around a coffee table? On the whole, the more relaxed the interview, the more useful information you will obtain from the candidate. To help you concentrate on what is being said make sure that there are no interruptions. Unplug the telephone if necessary.

CONDUCTING THE INTERVIEW

If you have a receptionist, make sure she knows that an interviewee will arrive. It is so unnerving to be met with a blank look when you arrive for an interview. Try to arrange for tea or coffee to be available – this can often ease the tension.

Start off by discussing unthreatening subjects such as whether the applicant found your offices easily. Try to establish some kind of rapport and relax the interviewee as much as you can – many will be extremely nervous, even though they manage to hide it.

Experience suggests that most employers make their decision whether or not to recruit during the first four minutes of an interview. It is only human nature to judge by first impressions, but do try to fight it – applicants deserve longer than this for such an important matter.

Assessing the applicant

If you are well prepared you will know exactly what you want to ask the candidate – but don't let it become too much like an interrogation! Listen carefully to what the applicant has to say; delve where necessary and show that you are interested by giving encouraging nods and remarks.

Every question you ask an applicant needs to try and establish:

- whether the person has the **ability** to do the job;
- whether the person is **honest**;
- whether the person is **stable**;
- whether the person will be **pleasant** to work with.

The way you pose your questions can make all the difference to the information you receive in return. Have a look at this example of how *not* to interview:

Interviewer   I see from your application form that you are working at Simpsons at the moment?

Applicant	Yes.
Interviewer	Do you enjoy it?
Applicant	Yes.
Interviewer	But you want to leave.
Applicant	Yes, that's right.
Interviewer	So you are a typist there, then?
Applicant	Er, yes.

Here the interviewer is asking a string of **closed questions**. Closed questions are ones where the interviewee can get away with just 'Yes' or 'No' answers. This is very hard work for the interviewer and he does not achieve much to show for it. He is also committing the cardinal sin of repeating back to the applicant what has already been stated on the application form! Note too that this interviewer ducks the issue – why doesn't he ask *why* the applicant wants to leave the current job?.

The interviewer would extract much more information if he asked open questions, those which demand more than 'Yes' or 'No' as an answer:

- What?
- Which?
- Why?
- When?
- Where?
- Who?
- How?

Here is a better attempt at the interview:

Interviewer	I see that you are working at Simpsons at the moment. **What** do they do?
Applicant	They are a large insurance broker and I work in the typing pool.
Interviewer	**Which** aspects of the job do you enjoy most?
Applicant	Well, it is very busy – and I like that. There is no chance to become bored.
Interviewer	So **which** aspect do you enjoy least?
Applicant	None really. The job's fine.
Interviewer	Then can you tell me **why** you are wanting to leave the job?
Applicant	It's my boss. I can't get on with her. She is forever interfering with my work. I've been there five

	years now – I don't need to be told what to do.
Interviewer	Can you give me some examples of **how** you think she interferes?
Applicant	She often stands over me while I work. It puts me off. She is very critical when I make mistakes.
Interviewer	**Why** do you have a problem accepting her authority?
Applicant	I don't really respect her because she is younger than I am and I've been at Simpson's longer. I should have had that job myself.
Interviewer	Have you any theories as to **why** you were passed over for promotion?

The dialogue above is much more informative, because the interviewer uses **open questions**. The interviewer is really getting to know the applicant – and the possible problems she could bring if she were employed. The interviewer is asking some pretty tough questions here, too – no shying away from awkward topics!

Here are just a few examples of open questions which you might want to ask at some stage in the interview:

- What do you hope to gain from a job change at this time?
- What made you apply for this job?
- What has been your greatest achievement at work?
- Why do you want to change your job?
- Why do you think we should employ you?
- Why did you decide that you wanted to work in this field?
- Where do you see yourself working in five years time?
- Who has influenced you most in your career?
- How did you achieve that?
- How much are you earning?
- How would you get to work each day?

The interviewer should not do most of the talking – 30% is really a maximum! Your job is merely to guide the interviewee into talking about the right things whilst you listen and analyse!

Sometimes hypothetical questions are useful – but only if the interviewee has had sufficient experience to give a worthwhile reply. For instance you could ask, 'How would you cope if a customer came in with a complaint and was clearly very irate?' Use such questions sparingly, as inexperienced interviewees can find them very threatening.

It would probably be much more effective to ask, 'Have you ever had to cope with irate customers in the past?... What did you do?' When asked hypothetical questions interviewees will try to give you the 'right answer', or tell you what they hope they would do. When asked 'What *did* you do?' you will be told how applicants have acted in the past – and that is generally the best indication of how they will act in the future.

Questions And Answers

Help! The applicant seems to be taking the interview over. What can I do?

The applicant could be extremely nervous or just a very forceful character. If you have been drinking coffee in a relaxed manner you could move back behind your desk for the rest of the interview. This may re-establish you authority!

Ask the applicant closed questions – those which can be answered in a word. If the applicant is rambling on, interrupt him: 'Good, that's interesting, Mr Green, but now I would like to move on to ask you about ...' Be firm!

If the applicant is really bumptious try to wind up the interview fairly quickly – it's unlikely you will want to employ him!

I become very nervous about interviewing – how can I overcome it?

Interviewing can be very nerve-racking. But bear in mind that the interviewee will probably be even more nervous than you are.

The best remedy for interview nerves is to be well prepared. Know exactly what you want to find out about each applicant, bearing in mind the demands of the job you want to fill. Keep to the structure of the interview and have a list of questions prepared so you will always have something to ask the interviewee. When those are covered, tell the applicant about the job and give *him* a chance to ask *you* questions.

Telling the applicant about the job

It is best to leave this part of the interview until after you have questioned the applicant. This way the applicant does not have a chance to match his answers to what he knows about the job.

Remember when talking about your company to 'sell it'. You want the applicant to be enthusiastic about joining your company. After all, the applicant may have several other interviews so you may be in competition with other employers. However, avoid misrepresenting the job at all costs. It is a recipe for future problems if you raise expectations unrealistically.

Here are the topics you should cover:

- The company – What it does, how long it has been established, its size, how successful it is, future developments.
- The job – Using the job description, discuss all aspects of the work. Its function within the business. Prospects.
- The package – Salary, holidays, sickness payments, etc.

At this stage give the applicant an opportunity to ask any questions. The questions asked will give you further insight into his or her personality and will show you whether they did any preparation for the interview!

Telling the applicant when to expect the result

A question which will be very much on the mind of the candidate is, 'When will I hear whether or not I've got the job?' so before the end of the interview clarify this point.

MAKING UP YOUR MIND

Firstly, and most importantly, *do not settle for the best of a bad bunch*. If you are not entirely happy about appointing one of your interviewees – don't. It is far better to start the process again. It will save you much time and money in the long run.

You will automatically have compared and contrasted applicants during the interview process and at the end of the final interview your decision will probably have been made. If you have doubts you can of course call one or two back for a second interview.

How to make a job offer

The delight and enthusiasm with which most jobs are accepted make this one of an employer's more rewarding tasks!

It can save a great deal of time if you telephone the applicant at home and informally offer the job. You can then find out, without delay, whether your offer is acceptable and you can agree a starting date. You can then prepare a letter of offer.

In this letter you set out most of the major terms and conditions of employment. The letter should give the following information:

- The job title.
- Where the job holder will work.
- The salary – amount, frequency of payment, and if appropriate details of overtime, shift allowances, commission, expenses, or car.
- The hours of work.
- Holidays.
- Provisos – References? Medical? Successful completion of a probationary period? Relocation? Car ownership? Telephone?
- Commencement details – date, time and where to report.
- You could enclose two copies of the job description. One for the employee to sign and return to you, the other for him to keep.

Sample letter offering employment

Dear Miss Knight,

I have pleasure in offering you the position of Sales Office coordinator to commence on Monday 9th February 19.. Please report to my office at 9.00 am.

This position carries a salary of £8,500 per annum, rising to £9,000 after the successful completion of the probationary period which shall not exceed three months.

Your hours of work will be from 9.00 am to 5.30 pm. Overtime, at a rate of time and a half, may be required occasionally. You will be entitled to 20 days paid holiday per annum, in addition to statutory holidays.

This offer is made subject to the provision of satisfactory references. Please would you send me details of whom we may approach for these, along with written acceptance of this offer.

I am looking forward to your joining the company and I hope that you will spend many happy years with us.

Yours sincerely, etc.

Rejection

Rejecting candidates is not a pleasant task but is best carried out as quickly as possible to minimize the applicants' anxious wait. However, don't reject really strong contenders for the position until the position has been accepted by your first choice.

This is the sort of letter to send to rejected applicants:

Dear Mr. Thomas,

Further to your recent interview for the position of Sales Administrator, I regret to inform you that, in this instance, your application has been unsuccessful.

I would like to take this opportunity to thank you very much for your interest in the company and I wish you every success in your search for a new position.

Yours sincerely, etc.

In cases where you were impressed with the applicant and there is a real possibility that there will be further vacancies in the future, you can include a paragraph such as:

I was impressed with your application for this position and would like to keep your details on file. I will contact you should a suitable vacancy arise in the near future.

You may now have solved a future recruitment problem too!

References

It really is worth taking up references. If you have put such a proviso in the job offer, and a nasty surprise emerges, it is not too late to back out.

Always ensure that you have the **applicant's consent** before taking up references.

A letter and brief form is a convenient way of asking for the information you require. Don't forget to enclose a stamped, addressed envelope.

Dear Sir or Madam,

Re. Miss T. Knight

The above-named has applied to us for the position of Sales Office Coordinator and has given your name as a referee. I should be very grateful if you would complete the details below and return the form to me as soon as possible. I assure you that any information given by you will be treated in confidence.

Yours faithfully, etc.

Name Miss T. Knight

1. Dates of employment. From ....
                        To ....
2. Job Title ....
3. Why did the applicant leave your employment?
   ....
   ....
   ....
4. Was the applicant:
   Honest? ....
   Punctual? ....
   Reliable? ....
   Conscientious? ....
5. Did the applicant have a good attendance record?
   ....
6. Would you re-employ the applicant?
   ....
7. Any other comments? ....
   ....
   ....

Signature ....
Date ....
Position ....
Company ....

Make sure that you do indeed treat the replies with strict confidence. A great deal of trouble can arise from tactless handling of references. Suppose you told an applicant that you were not taking him on because you have been told that he drinks too much, it could result in the applicant taking legal action against the ex-employer, who told you in good faith.

If you do receive a bad reference, and don't want to proceed with the job offer, it is best to send a letter. Say that you asked for satisfactory references but were unable to obtain them. You are therefore, regretfully, withdrawing your offer of employment. Avoid further comment.

Giving References

At some stage you will be on the receiving end of a reference request, and perhaps we should consider here how to handle them.

If all is well with an applicant, clearly you needn't hesitate in giving a glowing reference:

Dear Sir or Madam,

I confirm that Mr. Simmons was employed by us as a Clerical Assistant from 3.6.83 until his resignation on 3.3.89. Mr. Simmons was a loyal and conscientious employee and we were sorry to see him go.

I have no hesitation in recommending him to you as an employee.

Yours, etc.

But what if there have been problems? If so, in view of the liabilities, it is best to send a brief letter like this:

Dear Sir or Madam,

I confirm that Mr. Green was employed by us as a Clerical Assistant from 4.7.88 until the termination of his employment on 9.11.88.

Yours, etc.

Employers will be able to read between the lines and a telephone call may well follow. Then you may be more frank if you are assured that they will treat any information given in strict confidence.

CHECKLIST

Before the interview

- Do the candidates you have shortlisted for interview broadly fit the employee specification?
- Have you prepared for the interview fully?
- Have you allowed enough time for the interview?
- Have you ensured that you will not be interrupted?

During the interview

- Are you asking open questions?
- Is the applicant doing at least 70% of the talking?
- Are you getting all the information you need to make the best decision?
- Have you described the company and the job fully to the applicant?
- Has the applicant had ample opportunity to ask questions?

Tying things up

- Has the best applicant definitely accepted the job?
- Have you sent off for references?
- Have you rejected the rest? – those interviewed and those not?

4
Induction and Contracts

Although you have chosen the applicant whom you believe will be the best for the job you cannot expect him to be fully effective from day one. The new employee will go through an anxious, although hopefully exciting, period in which the job is learned and the surroundings and people become familiar.

INDUCTION

Induction ('leading in') should be a planned introduction to the company and job which helps a starter settle in as quickly as possible. Induction is not merely a matter of 'being nice' to a new employee; it makes sound business sense, too. The sooner an employee feels he belongs, the sooner he will be able to make a positive contribution to the business.

Some employees do not stay long in a new job. This is often called the **induction crisis**. Perhaps it would be better named the lack of induction crisis! It can happen because they have not been given sufficient guidance during those crucial first weeks.

Here are ten areas which should be covered in an informal induction session:

1. Introduction to other employees.
2. A tour of the building, including fire exits, washrooms and any other facilities.
3. Health and Safety regulations.
4. Company rules.
5. Details of wages or salary payment – when and how.
6. Collect the information you need from the employee in order to

pay him (usually P45, NI Number and bank details).
7. What to do when ill, ie ring in before a certain time.
8. Note details of whom to contact in case of an emergency.
9. Go through Job Description and discuss the stages in which the job will be learned and put into practice.
10. Put into action a job-related training programme.

Induction is not completed once you have covered all these: you will need to maintain a continuing interest in the employee's progress and make the employee feel welcome to come to you with any difficulties.

ACAS publishes a useful advisory booklet, number 7 in their series, called *The Induction of New Employees*. It is obtainable from any of their offices.

ACAS Head Office
11-12 St. James's Square
London SW1Y 4LA
(01) 214 6000

THE WRITTEN CONTRACT OF EMPLOYMENT

An employment contract is legally in existence from the moment an employee accepts an offer of work in return for wages. The law dictates (in the Employment Protection (Consolidation) Act of 1978) that a statement of the main terms and conditions of employment must be put **in writing** and given to an employee within thirteen weeks of starting work.

You need not go into great detail in the statement, but the following terms must be included:

- The names of the employer and employee.
- The date of commencement.
- The job title.
- The salary or rate of pay.
- The frequency of payment.
- The hours of work, including meal breaks.
- Holiday entitlement including public holiday arrangements.
- Payment arrangements for holiday periods.
- Sickness – what the employee must do; payment.
- Disciplinary rules.
- Disciplinary procedures.
- Grievance procedures.
- Pension arrangements (if you do not have any this must be stated).

- Notice to be given on either side.

Note Legislation is being proposed which will exempt employers of less than 20 people from providing employees with written particular of any disciplinary procedures which may apply.

Notice

You may specify any notice period you wish, as long as it is in excess of the **statutory minimum**. This is one week by the employee to the employer, if employed for any length of time exceeding a month.

In the case of the employer to the employee it is one week after the first month of employment, two weeks after two years and an additional week thereafter for each year's service up to a maximum of twelve weeks.

The terms and conditions listed above are the **express terms** of the contract. There are however, in addition, **implied terms**. These are unlikely to appear on any contract but the courts have established that they exist nonetheless. These are:

- To maintain trust and confidence through cooperation.
- To act in good faith towards each other.
- To take reasonable care to ensure health and safety in the work place.

Employees' Statutory Rights

Furthermore, your employee will have **statutory rights** which cannot be altered or put aside by a contract of employment. These include:

- The right to have a **written statement**.
- The right to **notice** of termination.
- The right to be given **written reasons** for dismissal after six months' service.
- The right to receive an **itemized pay statement**.
- The right not to be **discriminated** against on the grounds of sex, marital status or race.
- The right to **equal pay** with members of the opposite sex carrying out similar work or doing work of equal value.
- The right to **maternity** benefits.
- The right to minimum pay and employment conditions if your business is covered by a **wages council,**
- The right for **deductions not to be made** from pay unless required by statute (ie PAYE, national insurance), unless it

is a contractual term, or unless a written agreement has been received from the employee.

- The right to **guarantee** payments in respect of days when there is no work available. (See Department of Employment leaflet No.9 *Guarantee Payments*.)
- The right to **redundancy pay** after two years of service.
- The right to a **safe** system of work.
- The right to statutory **sick pay**.
- The right to **time off** for public duties, trades union duties, activities and training (if you recognize a union), and to look for work if declared redundant.
- The right to belong to a **trade union**
- The right to be **transferred** automatically, on the same terms, if the business changes hands.
- The right not to be **unfairly dismissed**.

Employers are strongly advised to obtain legal help when compiling a statement of main terms and conditions.

The Department of Employment publishes a very useful booklet *Written statement of main terms and conditions of employment*, number 1 in their series. It is free and available from Jobcentres or HMSO.

QUESTIONS AND ANSWERS

What happens if I want to change an item in the contract later?

If you think you may need a certain flexibility from your employees, for instance in their hours or place of work, this is best written into the contract in the first place.

If you later wish to alter the contract of employment, you require the consent of the employee – preferably in writing. Changes *can* be imposed without this, provided there are sound business reasons, but these reasons may be contested should an employee claim that he has been **constructively dismissed**.

What happens if I don't supply a statement of main terms and conditions of employment?

If an employee has not received written particulars he may refer the matter to an **Industrial Tribunal**. Tribunals have the power to decide what particulars the written statement should have included.

If a statement has been received by the employee, but it is contested regarding its accuracy or completeness, either party may refer the matter to an Industrial Tribunal.

Breaches of contract cannot be decided by an Industrial Tribunal. If either employer or employee believe that they have suffered material loss due to a breach of contract they have recourse to the ordinary courts of law.

CHECKLIST

Induction

- Decided where the employee will sit?

- Got all the equipment the employee will need to do the job?

- Allocated sufficient time to devote to the new employee?

- Designed an induction programme appropriate to the job?

- Decided exactly what future training may be required?

Contracts of Employment

- Prepared a statement of main terms and conditions of employment?

- Does it include all the mandatory conditions?

- Will you need to write in a certain amount of flexibility?

- Do all staff, who have worked with you for more than thirteen weeks, have such a statement?

5
Keeping Personnel Records

By law every business must keep records concerning accidents, employees' tax and national insurance deductions, statutory sickness pay and maternity pay; these are discussed in other chapters. You will also find it essential to keep employee records for your own use. These would typically include personal information, employment details and absence records.

Your personnel records will give you information necessary for planning your workforce, and will help you to identify training needs now and in the future. Careful records on discipline are particularly important as they may have to support a decision to dismiss.

Personnel records can also help you to ensure that every employee is treated consistently and fairly.

GETTING ORGANIZED

Here are four golden rules!

1. Keep the number of forms and information stored to a minimum – you will never be able to find important information if files are full of little notes on scraps of paper! Do not duplicate information.

2. Keep the records accurately.

3. Keep the records up to date.

4. Keep the records confidential. Decide which staff, if any, are to have access. Keep the information under lock and key.

Employment Record

Name
_____

Address _____   Date of birth_____

_____   Telephone number_____

Marital status _____   Number of children _____

Emergency Contact_____

Address _____

Home tel.no _____   Work tel. no._____

National Insurance number_____

Bank Address _____

Account number _____   Sorting Code _____

Holiday entitlement _____   Sickness entitlement ____

Starting date   Position   Starting salary
_____   _____   _____

Date   Personnel Variation
_____   _____
_____   _____
_____   _____
_____   _____
_____   _____
_____   _____
_____   _____
_____   _____
_____   _____

Decide what form your records will take. I would recommend a simple system where you keep a cardboard folder for each member of staff in a secure filing cabinet. In this you would keep:

- The initial application form or CV.
- Employment details.
- Sickness records.
- Holiday records.
- Absence records such as unauthorized absence and lateness.
- Disciplinary record.
- Details of accidents.
- Training records – including photocopies of relevant certificates.
- Copies of any letters you have sent to the employee – such as the offer letter and warning letters.
- Copies of any letters you have received from the employee – for instance the acceptance letter and grievance letters.
- Copies of any letters you have received about the employee – for example references, notes from the doctor and building society requests for salary information.

Personnel forms

You will of course need to keep a record concerning each employee's employment with you. This should include details of the position to which the employee has been appointed, the date of commencement, rate of pay and so on. Also note subsequent changes in employment, such as pay increases and promotions. Remember to record changes in addresses and emergency contacts.

You could make up a form like the one opposite.

A chart on your wall could be used as a register to get an overall picture of the extent of absences and to ensure that holidays do not coincide. Charts which can be used for this purpose are available from most office stationers.

'... and I had a shocking sore throat ...'

Employee Absence Record – 19....

Name _____ Position _____

Date   Reason for absence

_____   _____

_____   _____

_____   _____

_____   _____

_____   _____

_____   _____

_____   _____

_____   _____

_____   _____

_____   _____

_____   _____

_____   _____

_____   _____

_____   _____

_____   _____

_____   _____

_____   _____

_____   _____

_____   _____

_____   _____

	January																		
	1	2	3	4	5	6	7	8	9	10	11	12	13	14	15	16	17	18	19
	M	T	W	T	F	S	S	M	T	W	T	F	S	S	M	T	W	T	F
M. Smith	BH					/	/			B			/	/	De				
S. Brown	BH	A	L			/	/						/	/					
B. Green	BH	H	H	H	H	/	/	H	H	H	H	H	/	/					
G. Mills	BH				S	/	/			Op			/	/	C	C			
M. White	BH	S	S	Hp		/	/				Dr		/	/					TU

In this example — of a particularly disastrous three weeks – the key is as follows:

BH	Bank holiday	Dr.	Doctor	HP	Hospital
H	Holiday	Op	Optician	C	Training course
A	Absence	De	Dentist	B	Bereavement
S	Sick	L	Lateness	TU	Trades Union activities

QUESTIONS AND ANSWERS

I don't want to have to produce my own Personnel Forms. What are the alternatives?

There are several companies which publish standard personnel forms if you want a more professional image. For instance:

Waterlow Business Supplies
Oyez House
16 Third Avenue
Denbigh West Industrial Estate
Bletchley
Milton Keynes MK1 1TE
(0908) 71111

Formecon Publishing
Douglas House
Gateway
Crewe CW1 1YN
(0270) 500800

Croner's Personnel Records is a useful guide in a ring binder. This gives you up to date employment information and includes full size forms which you are allowed to photocopy for your own use. It is updated annually and is available from:
Croner Publications Ltd
Croner House
London Road
Kingston-upon-Thames
Surrey KT2 6SR
(01) 547 3333

What about keeping records on computer?

If you are a computer buff, you may consider buying some software for running personnel records on your personal computer. But it isn't really worth it unless you have several members of staff.

If you do decide to keep computerized personnel records, you will have to **register** under the Data Protection Act. Under this Act employees have the right to access to any information you hold about them on computerized records. You will still need to keep a manual system as a backup.

There are also several principles which you will have to adhere to if you keep computerized personnel records. Further information is available from:

The Data Protection Registrar
Springfield House
Water Lane
Wilmslow
Cheshire SK9 5AX
(0625) 535777

CHECKLIST

- Have you prepared a folder for each member of staff?

- Have you got all the information you require?

- Are you keeping your records to a minimum?

- Keeping them accurately?

- Keeping them up to date?

- Keeping them confidential?

- Have you prepared an Application form?

- An Employment Record?

- An Absence Record?

6
Wages and Salaries

HOW MUCH TO PAY YOUR STAFF

The amount you decide to pay your staff is crucial. You will need to pay enough to attract, and retain, the right quality staff, bearing in mind too the rates paid for similar work in your area.

To get an idea of comparable rates you may be able to join a local employers' organization which shares this and other employment information. Or you may find that keeping an eye on 'Sits Vac' columns in the local newspaper will be enough to keep you abreast of the local wage rates. Advice is available from your local Jobcentre.

If you are losing several staff to companies who pay more, paying too little will prove a false economy in the long run. On the other hand, of course, it would be unwise to pay your staff too generously as this will increase your overheads unnecessarily – and ultimately this could affect the viability of your business. Another danger is that ineffective staff are likely to become permanent fixtures as they can't afford to look for another job!

As well as identifying 'the going rate for the job' you will also need to work out suitable **differentials** in payment between members of your staff – considering the skills needed to do the job and the value of the job to your business. With the advent of the **Equal Pay Act** you must be careful to pay men and women the same amount for similar jobs or work of equal value.

Another key question is of course – how much can you afford to pay? The wages bill is likely to be one of your largest outgoings, and you must not forget the hidden costs of employing staff, such as your national insurance contribution, holiday pay and possibly company sick pay, bonus, overtime and shift premiums. These could add another 30%, or more, to your real bill.

The amount you pay may be subject to agreement with a union, or perhaps you have to conform to minimum standards laid down by a Wages Council.

Wages Councils were set up to increase the minimum wages payable in a number of industries – of course you may pay your staff more than the minimum! **Wages inspectors** ensure that the conditions set by the Wages Council are honoured. Where it is felt that collective bargaining will be effective in setting the rates of pay, either unions or employers can apply to have the Wages Council for that industry abolished.

Once the amount you pay has been agreed it cannot be reduced without the agreement of the staff. If you do a claim of constructive dismissal could be made against you.

HOW TO PAY YOUR STAFF

Firstly you must decide which system of payment to choose. There are two main systems although they can be implemented in several different ways.

Payment based on time worked

You can set an **hourly rate** of pay. In manufacturing units these are often recorded by use of a **clock card** system. Not every hour worked by any one employee will necessarily be paid at the same rate – for instance you may pay overtime at time and a half or double time. Shifts may attract an extra allowance at a percentage of the hourly rate.

You may decide to pay a weekly wage for a working week of a set number of hours. Senior staff may be salaried, in which case they are paid monthly (which can help your cash flow!). Their salary is usually quoted as an annual figure.

The benefit of a system of payment based on time worked is that it is relatively simple to administer and you can forecast your wages bill fairly accurately. Employees also like to know exactly what they are going to be paid.

Payment for time does not take into account the *quality* of the work carried out. You can, however, make part of the annual wages review a **merit award**, on top of cost of living, which should achieve the same effect. Merit awards have the advantage of being able to reward qualities which are not easily measured, such as persistence, reliability and creativity. A drawback to merit awards is that they are inevitably rather subjective and can give rise to claims of favouritism and inconsistency.

Payment by results

Where pay is directly linked to performance it is to motivate the employee to work harder – and, where appropriate, more effectively. There are several pay systems based on performance; all are more complicated and expensive to administer than payment for time.

- Individual payment by results is particularly suited to piece-work or sales, where an individual's performance can easily be gauged. It can however lead to friction between employees.

- Group payment by results is where a bonus for good job performance is paid to a team of employees – either equally or in agreed ratios. This is effective when small groups are working closely together; it becomes less so if the group is large. In this case the employee cannot directly relate the work he has done to the bonus he receives. The system can cause problems when a member of the group fails to pull his or her weight.

- With **measured daywork** a higher rate is paid on condition that a high level of performance is maintained. In a **stepped measured daywork** scheme there is a series of targets from which an employee can choose – each having a rate of pay attached to it. With these schemes the employer can estimate staffing costs and the employee knows how much will be earned. There is however the problem of what to do when an employee consistently fails to meet target: if nothing is done the pay scheme will rapidly lose respect.

- In **plant and enterprise wide** schemes a bonus, linked to output, is received by all employees. Profit sharing is a form of this type of payment. Here the bonus is, naturally, related to the profit made by the company. Payment can be in cash or in shares.

ACAS publishes a useful free advisory booklet, number 3 in their series, *Introduction to Payment Systems*.

There are also two basic methods of payment to consider:

- Cash payment
- Cashless pay

In the past, manual workers had the statutory right to be paid in the 'coin of the realm'. This they lost when the Truck Acts were repealed and the Wages Act came into force. This is good news for employers. Dealing in large amounts of cash to pay staff in this manner has two major disadvantages:

- Security problems. These are always present when large amounts of cash are handled and they range from payroll robberies and wages snatches to employees being mugged. Theft within the company may also occur.

- Cost. This includes the cost of a security firm to deliver the cash if you have several employees, the wages of the person who has to make up the pay packets, plus steep bank charges. You may find that your cash flow will benefit from cashless pay. With cash payments you will need to withdraw the cash before the payment is due; but in an automated banking system payments are both debited and credited the same day. Your bank can advise you of a suitable method of arranging this for your business.

From the employee's point of view the advantages of cashless pay include better security, an encouragement to save, and greater ease in obtaining a loan or a mortgage. Nor are employees restricted to having bank accounts. Payments can easily be made straight into a building society where interest can be earned on current accounts. The disadvantages of cashless pay are, in some cases, lack of access to cash and bank charges for those unable to stay 'in the black'.

You can make it a condition of employment for new starters that they are paid directly into a bank or building society account. However care must be taken not to force existing employees currently paid in cash to change to cashless pay. It could be construed to be a major change to the terms of employment, and a constructive dismissal claimed.

A TAXING PROBLEM

From your first day as an employer the local inspector of taxes will need to know that you have become an employer, and will be particularly interested in hearing from you as a new source of revenue!

As an employer you have a duty to deduct income tax and national insurance contributions under the **PAYE (Pay As You Earn)** system for all employees earning over a minimum amount. This is usually reviewed annually. PAYE applies to employees whether they are paid weekly, monthly or at any other interval.

The responsibility to deduct tax and national insurance exists even if you have not been specifically requested to make these deductions – so pleading ignorance is no excuse! You will also have to account for these deductions to the collector of taxes at a later date, and tax inspectors are entitled to examine your records.

To operate PAYE you need to know your employee's **tax code**. This indicates the personal tax allowances to which the employee is entitled. The tax code, along with the national insurance number, will appear on **form P45** which new starters will give you. This details earnings and tax deductions for the tax year to date.

Tax tables, deduction working sheets for tax and national insurance and end of year return forms are all available from the tax office. Also ask your local Inspector of Taxes to send you a copy of *The Employer's Guide to PAYE* and *The Employer's Guide to National Insurance Contributions* which gives full details of what is required.

You will be able to trace your local inspector by looking in your local telephone directory under **Inland Revenue**. Your personal taxes may be handled at a different office from that dealing with your business.

National insurance

National insurance, along with taxation, provides the funds necessary to run the social security system. Every employee earning over the lower earnings limit, a figure usually changed annually, must pay national insurance contributions.

Not only must you deduct national insurance for each employee, but you have to pay an employer's contribution, too. This contribution is also payable for every employee earning above the lower earnings limit

If you have an occupational pension scheme which satisfies certain conditions you can contract your employees out of part of the state scheme, which means that you pay lower contributions.

Contact your local DSS office for more details. You will find this under **Social Security, Department of** in the telephone book.

QUESTIONS AND ANSWERS

I have heard that there are some employees for whom I do not have to deduct tax and national insurance. Who are they?

Firstly there are those employees, who have already been mentioned, who are earning below a certain limit.

Tax and national insurance need not be deducted from 'casual employees' who are in your employ for a week or less and who are earning less than the PAYE threshold. In these cases you need only record their names and addresses and the amount you have paid them.

In the case of students, tax need not be deducted as long as the student and employer make a declaration on form P38(S). This has to be returned at the end of the tax year along with your annual statement, declaration and certificate (a P35).

Tax and national insurance is not deducted from Employment Training and Youth Training Scheme trainees.

If any of the people working for you are self-employed it will be their responsibility to make arrangements for tax and national insurance deductions.

National insurance is not paid by employees under 16 or over pensionable age. In the latter case a certificate of age exemption (CF384) or a certificate of earner's non-liability (CF381) should be obtained by the employee from a Social Security office and the form kept by you.

Is it legal to make any deductions from employee's wages, apart from PAYE and national insurance?

The rules governing other deductions are strict and laid out in the Wages Act 1986. No deduction may be made unless:

- It is a 'relevant provision' of the employee's contract of employment. The employee must have had a copy or written notification of this.
- The employee has given written permission to the employer for the deduction to be made.

There are additional regulations covering retail workers. Employers may seek to recover cash or stock shortages from employees wages. In this case the deductions must comply with the rules above and in addition:

- The deduction must not represent more than 10% of the wages.
- The loss must have arisen from dishonesty, the conduct of the employee or some other event for which the employee has contractual liability.
- The employer must write to the worker stating his or her total liability in respect to the loss and must have demanded payment in writing.

Overpayment of wages is not covered by the Wages Act, nor are deductions which are to be made to satisfy a court or tribunal order – for example, an attachment of earnings order.

If an unauthorized deduction is made from an employee's wages he may complain to an industrial tribunal.

RECORDS

You will need to keep a **wages book** to summarize the weekly and monthly wage payments. There are several suitable books produced commercially and your accountant will probably recommend one.

Computer software is available for running wages systems. Should you decide to use one purely for these purposes you will not, currently, have to register under the Data Protection Act.

Pay slips
Each employee is entitled, by law, to receive an **itemized pay slip** for each payment made. It must include the following information:-

- The gross amount of the wages or salary
- Deductions, including PAYE, national insurance, and possibly saving plans and union dues.
- The net amount of the wages or salary.
- The amount and method of payment where it is paid by more than one means, for instance part into the employee's bank account and part in cash.

Wages envelopes are available from business stationers; they usually include an adequate summary.

Full information is available in the Department of Employment's booklet *Itemized Pay statements*. This is available free from Jobcentres.

PAYMENT OF STAFF WHO ARE ABSENT

Holidays
Generally speaking there is no statutory requirement for you to grant holidays, bank holidays or give holiday pay. An exception is bank holidays for young people working in factories.

However if you are thinking of not granting paid holidays to your staff do bear in mind that there is competition between employers for high quality staff. If you do not give your staff an adequate holiday entitlement you will find that you will lose the best to more generous employers. The staff which remain with you will be those who can't find another job!

Your terms and conditions relating to these topics must appear on the written statement of main terms.

Statutory Sick Pay

Apart from holiday entitlement the majority of payments you make for staff who are absent will be for sickness.

Even if you do not have a company sick pay scheme most employees, however recently they have joined you, will be entitled to some payment. This payment is called Statutory Sick Pay (SSP).

The employees who do *not* have this statutory right are those who—

- Are ill outside the EEC countries.
- Are ill during an industrial dispute.
- Are over pensionable age.
- Are earning less than the national insurance lower earnings limit.

All other employees are entitled to payment, based on gross earnings, for up to 28 weeks of any period of incapacity for work. After that they would be transferred to state benefit, if appropriate. SSP rates are usually revised annually.

Employees are entitled to SSP after a three day 'waiting period' in which no payment is accrued. So an employee has to be off work for a minimum of four **qualifying days** to receive any payment. Qualifying days are those on which an employee would normally work. This is a simple calculation for Monday to Friday employees, but becomes more complicated for staff working a rotating shift pattern.

If an employee is off work due to sickness, following a period of incapacity within the previous eight weeks, the two periods are linked and treated as one SSP period – so the three waiting days are not necessary for the subsequent absence. However this subsequent absence must also be of at least four days' duration for payment to be made.

After seven days' absence, including days which are not usually worked, a **medical certificate** from a doctor is required. Previous to that self-certification is sufficient.

The payments you make must be carefully recorded and kept for three years. The DSS may want proof that you are administering the scheme properly. SSP is to be treated as earnings for national insurance and PAYE purposes – so contributions will have to be made where appropriate. SSP payments will be reimbursed to you via reductions in your employers's national insurance contributions.

Full details about administering the Statutory Sick Pay are available in the DHSS booklet *Employer's Guide to Statutory Sick Pay.*

If you feel that an employee is abusing the sickness scheme – that is to say malingering – disciplinary action may be necessary. In some cases SSP payments can be withheld.

Company sick pay

At some stage, if you can afford it, you may consider introducing your own sick pay scheme for your employees. This is often known as **occupational sick pay**.

There are disadvantages of not having an occupational sick pay scheme – other than the obvious one suffered by your employees! Employees may come into work when they are ill – this is likely to hinder their recovery and they may even spread their illnesses. In addition you are more likely to be able to attract and retain employees if you have a scheme. Never forget that you are competing with large companies for the best staff.

Occupational sick pay schemes vary considerably in the amount paid, the period of service before entitlement and the length of entitlement.

You would be well advised to consult other local employers before proceeding with your own plans.

You will also need to decide whether or not visits to doctors, dentists and opticians may be taken in paid company time.

OTHER PAYMENTS TO STAFF WHO ARE ABSENT

Whether you grant time off with pay for bereavement, moving house, marriage and even paternity is solely at your own discretion. It is a good idea to clarify your thoughts on this so that you are not forced into an 'instant decision' by an employee. A stated policy on these absences will also ensure consistency.

There are some absences which you must, by law, allow your staff. Some of these do not have to be paid and some do:

Unpaid absences – public duties

- Staff who are Justices of the Peace.
- Staff who are members of a local authority.
- Staff who are members of a statutory tribunal.

- Staff who are members of a regional or district Health Authority (Health Board in Scotland).
- Staff who are members of a water authority (River Purification Board in Scotland).
- Staff who are school or college governors.

Paid time off

- Reasonable amounts of time off for all staff engaged in union activities.
- Reasonable amounts of time off for union representatives for union duties and training.
- Reasonable amounts of time off for health and safety representatives, for duties and training.
- Reasonable amounts of time off for employees under notice of redundancy to either look for a new job or arrange training.
- Reasonable amounts of time off for pregnant employees to receive ante-natal care.

Jury service

There are no regulations stating whether or not you should pay your staff whilst they attend for jury service. Staff may claim allowances for travel, subsistence and financial loss, from the courts.

Territorial Army

There is no statutory basis for granting time off to employees involved in the Territorial Army, since attendance is voluntary. So whether you grant time off in excess of holiday entitlement, and whether that time off is paid, is entirely at your discretion.

A HAPPY EVENT?

The law which protects pregnant women at work, provides them with pay, and in some cases gives them the right to return to work, is a great step forward for women in employment – but it does give the employer quite a few headaches. Take a deep breath – this whole section on maternity might make heavy reading!

Employees with **more than two years' continuous service** with the company may have:

- the right to return (with exceptions);
- the right to Statutory Maternity Pay (SMP);

- the right not to be dismissed by reason of their pregnancy;
- the right to paid time off for ante-natal care from a doctor; midwife or health worker. (You are advised to request evidence of these appointments.)

The right to return

If, immediately before the employee's maternity leave begins you have fewer than five employees, failure to permit her to return to her job after maternity leave will *not* be classed as a dismissal. The law recognises that for small businesses the inconvenience of keeping a job open for the length of maternity leave would be quite great. Larger companies, who do have to keep the job open, often appoint temporary staff to fill the gap.

To have the right to return your employee must have had at least two years' continuous service in your company, working more than sixteen hours per week. If she works fewer than sixteen hours, but at least eight hours per week, she must have worked for you, continuously, for at least five years to have the right to return.

The employee must inform you, in writing, at least twenty-one days before the leave commences that:

- she will be absent due to maternity;
- she intends to return to work after maternity leave;
- the date her baby is due to be born.

For entitlement to return she may leave at any time after the beginning of the eleventh week before the baby is due. She may return to work at any time she wishes before the end of the twenty-ninth week after the baby is born. This may be postponed for up to four weeks if a doctor's certificate is supplied.

If you write to the employee seven weeks (or more) after the baby is born, asking her to decide whether or not she wishes to return, she must let you know, in writing, within 14 days of receiving the letter, if she wishes to return.

Statutory Maternity Pay

There are two rates of Statutory Maternity Pay (SMP). Which is to be paid depends upon the employee's length of service.

To qualify for the **higher rate** of SMP she must:

- Have been **employed by you continuously** for two years for sixteen or more hours per week (or five years if working between eight and sixteen hours per week) by the time she reaches fifteen weeks before the baby is due to be born. This fifteenth week is known as the 'qualifying week'.

- Still be **pregnant eleven weeks** before the baby is due – or have had the baby by that time. That is to say she has not miscarried or had a still birth by that time.

- Have **ceased work** due to pregnancy.

- Have given you **medical evidence** that she is pregnant. A photocopy of the form called a *MAT B1* will be given to her by the midwife or doctor and this shows the date on which the baby is expected.

- Give you 21 **days' notice in writing** that she will be leaving due to maternity, to be entitled to SMP. This applies even if the employee does not wish to return to work, or she does not have the right to return.

- Have average earnings high enough for her to pay **national insurance contributions**.

If the employee meets all these conditions she is entitled to maternity pay for a total of eighteen weeks, as long as she has given up work by the sixth week before the baby is due. Maternity payments cannot start until the eleventh week before the baby is born.

The higher rate of SMP is paid for the first six weeks of this eighteen week period. This rate is nine-tenths of her average weekly earnings over the eight weeks which end on the pay day immediately before the end of the 'qualifying week'.

During the remaining twelve weeks of maternity pay she will be paid SMP at the lower rate, the amount of which is usually revised annually.

The lower rate of SMP is payable to employees, irrespective of the number of hours they work, with over six months' but under two years' continuous service at the fifteenth week before the baby is due. Apart from this, the same rules apply to qualify for this rate as for the higher rate.

Full details about SMP are given in the DSS booklet *Employer's Guide to Statutory Maternity Pay*.

LEAVERS

When a contract of employment comes to an end it is usually by one of the parties giving **notice**. However in exceptional circumstances, such as summary dismissal or repudiation of the contract, notice is not given, nor is it paid.

The notice period given by the employer or employee must follow that stated in the contract of employment, or be the minimum stated in law.

If you dismiss an employee, you can if you wish give **payment in lieu of notice** (PILON). These payments are not usually subject to PAYE. PILON payments are also often made when an employee has resigned, but you decide that the risk involved in letting the employee work the notice period is too great. For instance, if someone wanted to set up in competition with you he could spend the notice period gathering useful information!

If, during a notice period which was to be worked, employees are ready and willing to work but none is given, or if they are on holiday or sick, they must be paid a week's pay for each week of their statutory notice entitlement. Sickness benefit can be taken into account when calculating the week's pay.

If work continues normally during the notice period, normal payment is given.

When an employee leaves a *Details of Employee Leaving* form (P45) must be completed. This shows the total pay (less any pension contributions) earned during the current tax year until the date of leaving. It also records the total amount of tax which has been deducted. Don't fill up the P45 until the final payment has been made.

Retirement and pensions

Occasionally an employee will leave you to retire. The widely recognised ages are 60 for women and 65 for men. However under the Sex Discrimination Act women who wish to work up until 65 may do so, if that is the retirement age for men in the same company. So employers can no longer set different retirement ages for men and women.

This does not affect a woman's right to a state or occupational pension if she wishes to retire at 60.

Following recent legislation there has been a great deal of interest in pensions. The government are encouraging individuals and their employers to provide for their own pensions. There is little scope for increasing state pensions – people are living longer and fewer are working to fund the scheme.

Currently there are three types of pension:

- SERPS – the State Earnings Related Pension Scheme.

- Personal pension schemes.
- Occupational (company) pension schemes.

There are advantages to setting up a company pension scheme. It can help you recruit and retain good staff. It can give your company a caring image and be a tax effective benefit to give.

There are several schemes available for small businesses which are worth investigating if you are an established employer.

CHECKLIST

- Have you gathered sufficient information to set realistic and competitive rates of pay for your staff?

- Have you decided whether to pay them for time worked, or by results?

- Will you be paying your staff in cash, or directly into their bank/building society accounts?

- Do the tax office and DSS know that you are about to become an employer?

- Have you set up a system of administration for wages – including the provision of itemized pay slips for employees?

- Have you obtained full details and paperwork necessary for the administration of SSP and SMP?

- Have you decided you own policy on holiday pay? Occupational sick pay? Bereavement? Other absences?

7
Effective Staff Management

The art of good management is to achieve your objectives *through the effective use of other people.*

Companies focusing merely on figures and numbers tend to believe that their workforce consists of individuals who work only for the money. They may assume that the staff have no initiative and do not expect job satisfaction. Such businesses usually have a very autocratic style of management guaranteed to destroy any constructive team spirit – the staff will only be united in their conflicts with the management! Such a company culture encourages greed and unrest.

The other extreme is the company where everyone is happy but nothing much is achieved! Many managers make the mistake of wanting to be liked by all – but end up being respected by none.

A fine balance is required to ensure achievement by motivated and enthusiastic staff. If you can achieve a combination of caring for your staff and concentration on the job to be done, both staff and organization will gain.

In this chapter we shall look at some key management skills, including:

- time management and organisation
- assertiveness
- delegation
- motivation
- leadership
- counselling

All of these demand a great deal of skill from managers and often a change in their behaviour – not always easy when it is your own

67

business and there are so many extra pressures on you.

HELP, I HAVEN'T GOT TIME!

Until you are organized yourself, it will be very difficult, if not impossible, for you to organize other people.

Even if you do have several employees you will often find that your own workload seems to be too great for one person to handle and that there isn't enough time to do all that you would wish. Time is a resource just like any other you use in your business. The old adage 'Time is money' is as true as ever it was, so the use of this valuable resource must be planned carefully. This is called **time management**.

- **Value of planning**
  The first principle of time management is to accept that time spent planning is not wasted, but is the most constructive way in which to use it. Planning your time is an investment because it will save you time in the future. Job schedules which allow plenty of time for planning tend to take less time in total than those which have not been carefully planned.

- **Your action list**
  When planning, it is important not to keep too much information in your head, for two reasons; firstly you may forget it, and secondly it is when you are trying to remember all that there is to do that you are most likely to feel swamped or panic! So a 'things to do' list is an essential, if not *the* essential, piece of paper on your desk.

- **Prioritise**
  Once everything is down on paper you can evaluate and prioritise the items. Some things will be important but not urgent; others will be urgent but not important; a few will be both, or neither. Looking at the list you can decide what you will do first. The trivial things can be put at the bottom of the list or even deleted.

- **Book time with yourself**
  Don't just use your diary to note business appointments and meetings; use it to make appointments with yourself! Block off parts of the week and reserve them to get on with important tasks, like planning. It will never get done if everyone else uses up your time!

- **Resist distractions**
  It is important not to let several 'five minute' jobs take up all your day – it is so tempting to get them out of the way first so that you can get on with the big jobs with a clear conscience. If you do that there never seems to be quite time for the things which really matter.

- **Finish what you start**
  Attempt just one thing at a time and finish it, or progress it as far as you can, before moving on to something else. This is difficult, especially when you are running your own business and there are constant interruptions. These need to be controlled – learn to say 'no' nicely (see assertiveness!) and encourage your staff to make their own decisions (see delegation!).

- **Get rid of paperwork**
  Set aside the first half hour, or hour if necessary, to sorting out the post. Your most important piece of equipment here is *the waste paper basket*. Throw away as much as you can and pass on or answer the rest. **The secret is to only handle each piece of paper just once**. It is easy to leave a pile of unanswered mail piled on your desk which you intend to deal with 'sometime'. The letters in the pile have probably been picked up and read several times. Let your motto be 'Do it now!'

- **Keep your desk clear**
  Another secret of not feeling swamped is an uncluttered desk. Apart from your diary and your 'things to do' list, the only thing on your desk should be the job you are doing. With a list of outstanding jobs you need not worry that you will forget a job if it is not in sight.

- **Review yourself**
  Finally make sure that you review the way you are doing things regularly. For instance ask yourself:

  What am I doing? Why?
  Is there something *better* I could be doing?
  How am I doing it? Why?
  Is there a *better way* to do it?
  Why am *I* doing it?
  Would *someone else* be better?
  Where is it being done? Why?

Is it the best *place* for it to be done?

'DO IT MY WAY...?'

Properly used, assertiveness is one of the most useful management techniques! It is specially effective in the management of potential conflicts and it encourages others to behave reasonably.

Most people react to conflict with aggression or submission – it is all part of our 'fight or flight' instinct. However the first fails to recognise the rights of others and the second fails to recognise your own rights. In using assertion you recognise that both you and the other person have equally important interests.

Properly handled, assertive behaviour will mean that at the conclusion of an exchange there will be a solution acceptable to both parties; at worst there will be a compromise.

Here are three stages to follow in being assertive:

1. Say that you understand their position. Agree to some extent. Be sincere!
2. Say how you feel about the situation, for example: 'However, I feel...' or 'But I think...' Avoid using phrases like 'You must' or 'You should'.
3. Reach a mutually acceptable solution by asking questions and discussing the answers.

So how does assertiveness work in practice? Imagine yourself in the following scenario.

A highly irate Peter, your salesman, comes into your office, slams the door behind him and shouts:

'I've just heard that you are not making widgets next week! I don't believe it! The trouble with your production plans is that you are unable to fill the orders I win. You make us look stupid and incompetent... I've got to have 2,000 widgets for the end of next week – or we lose the customer. What are you going to do about it?'

How will you react? – Aggressively? Submissively? – or ~~ .c-ly?

● An example of an **aggressive** re~~
'Well, you sales pe~~ appreciation at all of the problems we~~ ~~duction! You ought to find out what c~~ is before you go around making promises~~ with a little foresight, you would know you ~~ ~p!'

This attracts further abuse until Peter storms out of your office again, still feeling angry and nowhere near solving his (or the firm's) problem. You are left fuming.

- Would a **submissive** response achieve more?
  'Oh dear, we've got a tight schedule at the moment and if we rearrange... well, I suppose I could drop the... but that would mean...'
  'I've got to have them.'
  'Oh...alright then.'
  'Great! Cheerio.'

  This has achieved a lot for Peter – but now you have a problem. What about all the customers waiting for the other products scheduled to be made? You can't let them have their own way, too!

- How about giving Peter an **assertive** response?
  'What is the problem, Peter?'
  'Well, I visited Marshall's today and you know how long I have been waiting for an order from *them*! He said if I could supply 2,000 widgets by the end of next week we could have the order. Their usual supplier can't come up with the goods for another month. This is our big chance – so obviously I said yes!'
  'I can understand how important this order is to you in that case (*stage one*), however I feel that it would be unwise to change our production schedule at such short notice because we would let down other important clients (*stage two*). I do have a slot the following week in which we could make Marshall's order. Do you think that would help?'
  'Umm... that should be alright because we shall still beat the competition. I'll ring Marshall's now and let you know definitely as soon as I can.' (*stage three*).
  By being assertive a workable compromise has probably been reached – with both parties giving a bit.
  Assertiveness is not easy, because when under attack from someone like Peter it is very hard not to let your hackles rise. Often it will require you to stick to your point during a long onslaught, in which case you have to calmly repeat your feelings, like a broken record, until the message is received and understood!

DELEGATION – OVER TO YOU!

One of the most difficult of management tasks is delegation. Most entrepreneurs find it hard to 'let go' and trust someone else to do a job. There are several reasons for this:

- They don't believe that anyone else can do the job as well.
- They believe that they can do everything themselves.
- They are worried about losing control of any aspect of the business.
- They regret giving up the jobs they enjoy.

All these reasons are understandable and sometimes justified. However, the expansion of your business will depend ultimately upon someone taking some of the load off your shoulders. Then you can concentrate on developing the areas *only you* can, such as planning. So do include a sensible division of the work so that each employee can get on with making his or her contribution without needing continual instructions from you.

So what exactly is delegation? It means:

- Entrusting part of your job to someone else.
- Giving them a specific objective to reach.
- Giving them the authority to make decisions without referring to you.
- Making sure they have enough knowledge and skill to carry out the task.

It is *not*:

- A chance to get rid of all the jobs you detest.
- An opportunity to abdicate accountability.
- Designed to let you put your feet up and read the paper.

In business your major tasks will include planning, organizing, analysing and motivating. Other functions may be suitable for delegation to others.

Of course, you can only delegate so far as a person is able to do a job; it is important that adequate training is given and that you are available for advice when needed.

When delegating do make it clear exactly what the responsibilities are. This should help your employees to avoid delays caused by uncertainty about whether they have the authority to act in a certain situation. It will also stop them from overstepping the mark! It is a good idea to put the key areas of the task in writing and, where possible, define what a good performance in the job would be.

It is important not to interfere with a job once you have delegated it – but do meet up regularly to evaluate how the work is progressing. Obviously mistakes will occur from time to time and to some extent you have to allow the employee the right to fail – the only people who do not make mistakes are those who don't do anything.

WHAT MAKES PEOPLE TICK?

We are all motivated by different needs depending upon circumstances and personality, but we all have certain basic needs which have to be fulfilled. The achievement of these basic needs is what motivates people first of all. Once these have been achieved they can set their sights higher. In 1943 Abraham Maslow identified a hierarchy of needs:

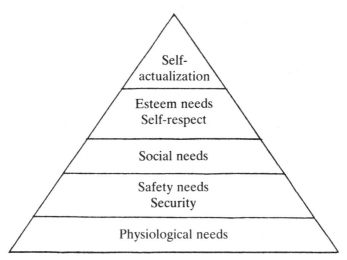

The basic level of need is at the foot of the triangle. These physiological needs include air, food, warmth and shelter. These needs clearly have to be fulfilled before we can have any greater ambition.

Once these physiological needs have been achieved one is motivated to retain them. So the next level in the hierarchy is security. This would include security of job and income and also explains why we have several different types of insurance policy and worry about our pension arrangements. Having once achieved security it can be lost again – for instance someone made redundant may return to the base of the pyramid in terms of his motivation. Once security has been achieved, however tenuous, it will no longer serve to motivate the individual and so the next level becomes a target.

This next level concerns social needs. To a greater or lesser extent we all need to be accepted by a peer group, and closely following this the next ambition is to be esteemed by them. Self regard also comes as a motivation at this level.

At the pinnacle of the pyramid is self-actualization, the development of one's potential to the full. This is achieved by just a few, hence its position at the tip of the pyramid.

By paying a wage you are probably providing for the physiological needs of your staff, and if your business thrives you will also be giving them a degree of security. Some employers assume that money is the only thing that motivates their staff. If you follow such a policy it will become a vicious circle. If money is the only thing on offer they will continually want more of it. Once one pay rise has been achieved it will no longer motivate and they will be looking for the next. By looking at the higher levels of motivation and helping their staff to achieve them, employers can avoid this trap to some extent.

Where you can motivate people beyond a need for cash is in the supply of their ego needs. Let your staff be aware of the contribution they make to the business. Let them see their efforts in the context of the whole, both as individuals and as a team.

Many people thrive on a little praise and recognition (don't all of us?) and this, given sincerely, will go a long way towards meeting your staff's ego needs.

Don't wait until appraisal time to congratulate your staff – do it whenever you see, or hear of, them doing something well. Tell them when a customer has made favourable comments about them. Be specific in your praise. Don't just say 'You are doing well – I am pleased with you,' but for example instead, 'Miranda, I'm very pleased with how well the new filing system you designed is working. I've been able to find things so much more quickly than I did before. Well done.'

You can also help your staff towards self-actualization through good use of delegation and training. Make it part of your job not only to recognise their successes but encourage them on to greater things. Give your staff a sense of direction and plenty of feedback, too.

TICKINGS OFF

Of course it won't always be sweetness and light. There are bound to be times when you need to give a member of staff a reprimand. Here we are not talking about offences calling for the dreaded 'disciplinary procedure', but more or less routine tickings ⟨ correct a small problem.

It is important not to shirk your role here – your staff have a right to know how they are performing. You tell them when they are doing well; tell them too when they are doing badly.

There is no point in getting into a state and shouting at an employee. If that's how you feel it is better to leave the reprimand until you have calmed down a bit. Make sure that you criticise the *behaviour*, not the person. The behaviour can be modified, the person can't!

When you need to talk to an employee about a matter of discipline it is important to do it in private. Don't whatever you do, humiliate your employee by chastising him or her in front of their colleagues.

Explain to the employee what has happened, tell them how you feel about it, pause and then... praise them! For instance 'I was particularly disappointed in your sales figures this month – because you are usually the top performer!' With luck they will leave determined not to let the side down again!

Use of assertive techniques can also help you to put your message across more effectively. Avoid being judgemental; stick to facts and give them a clear reason for changing their behaviour. For instance, don't say 'You are so careless in the way you run the stock records. Several figures are wrong!' Try 'I know that working with figures all day can be tiring, but I was disappointed to see how many mistakes have been made in these stock records. Mistakes will result in...'. This approach may result in advice being sought, such as 'Is there a better way I can approach this problem?' Whenever possible try to work out a solution together.

Of course, reaction to criticism, however carefully put, is likely to be hostile and there will be times when you have to put the employee straight more firmly.

FOLLOW THE LEADER!

A leader may be followed for many reasons – trust, respect, fear, awe of position, even charisma! Few of us can aspire to being charismatic leaders, so the best to aim for are trust and respect. Neither of these can be demanded from your staff – they can only be earned.

Build a strong team by *believing* that they are strong! Have confidence in them and never run them down. It helps to use the word 'we' when talking about tasks and goals. Hold regular meetings and make sure that everyone has a chance to make their point and ask several questions. You may be surprised how constructive it can be, especially when they start to bounce ideas off one another. Encourage them to take part in decision-making. You will find that a team is greater than the sum of its parts.

It is important to treat your staff equally – don't have favourites and don't victimise or ostracise anyone. Help everyone build a strong identity as a team working for a common goal – and, again, let everyone know how important their contribution is.

TEA AND SYMPATHY?

From time to time your employees will have personal problems which either affect their work or that they need to discuss with you.

Being cast in the role of counsellor can be extremely worrying until you realize how many problems are solved by merely offering a sympathetic ear. Giving employees a chance to talk around the problem often leads to them finding their own solutions. In fact it is wise *not* to impose a solution of your own devising.

Keep an eye open to spot problems; not all of your employees will want to make the first approach. When a problem becomes apparent set aside a time when you can talk privately without interruption. Be as informal as you can.

Encourage the person to talk by offering reassurance and encouragement, and by asking open questions – how? what? why? when? where? who? Help them talk through how they are feeling about the problem. It can help to show your own vulnerability – but spare them your own problems!

Listen carefully – and *show* that you have been listening by summarizing the points the employee makes. Avoid definite advice or criticism – if you have an idea which might help, just offer it as a suggestion. Suggestions about where to find qualified advice or help would be constructive.

When the staff have found their own solution, support it and agree with them the action they should take. Finally, let them know that they are welcome to have a further talk if they want to.

After the discussion act as if it never happened. *Never* betray the confidence the employee has entrusted in you.

CHECKLIST

Time management

- How often do you find yourself saying 'I haven't got time'?

- What percentage of your time do you spend planning?

- Do you make 'things to do' lists?

- If so, do you prioritize your tasks?

- Do you use your diary to make appointments with yourself, too?

- Do you do just one job at a time?

- When did you last see the top of your desk?

- Have you got a large enough waste paper basket?

- How good is your aim?

Being assertive

- Do you find yourself responding aggressively to attack?

- Do you find yourself giving in to other people's demands too often?

- Or are you assertive?

- Do you let others know that you understand their point of view?

- Do you say how you feel?

- Do you try to reach a mutually acceptable compromise?

Delegation

- Do you try to do *everything* yourself?

- Or do you delegate?

- Try to identify tasks which you could entrust to your staff:

   Which member of staff would be best for the job?
   What training will they require to be able to do the work?
   How much authority will you give them?
   What targets will you set?
   How often will you meet to review?

Telling staff when you are pleased...

- Do you notice when your staff do something well?

- Do you let them know that you are pleased?

- Do you praise them about a specific instance?

...and when you are not!

- Do you criticize the person – or just what they have (or haven't) done?

- Do you tick them off in private?

- Do you aim to agree a solution?

Leadership

- Do you have several individuals working for you, unaware of their role in the business as a whole – or do you have a team working for you towards a common goal?

- Do you keep your staff informed on how the business is developing?

- Do you ask the advice of your employees?

- Do you let them take part in decision-making when you can?

- Do you let them know that you value their contribution?

Counselling

- Do you discuss employee's problems in private, informally and without danger of interruption?

- Do you reassure them? Ask questions? Let them see that you are vulnerable too?

- Do you show that you have been listening to them by summarizing?

- Do you avoid imposing a decision, but instead try to lead them to make their own?

8
Staff Appraisal

Since staff are such a costly investment, you must be aware of what they are achieving for you as individuals. How well are they doing their jobs? What can you do to improve their performance?

A common way of assessing staff is by means of an **appraisal system**. This involves interviewing the staff individually, each year, to discuss aspects of their work – such as what they do well, where their weaknesses are, what needs improvement, how this can be achieved and where their future development lies.

Some managers respond to the idea of appraisals with dismay. 'I speak to Harry every day! Why on earth should we meet formally? I *know* how he is doing.' However, few managers do actually set aside time to discuss and consider each employee during a hectic working day. So it's a good plan to make a formal appointment. This has the benefit of giving the employee time to prepare for the meeting, too.

The interview should be a two-way discussion during which performance is measured against the job description. Plans of action, or targets, also need to be *agreed* – the appraisal must not become a 'telling' session!

But what will an appraisal scheme *achieve* for you?

WHY APPRAISE YOUR STAFF?

Ultimately all appraisals aim to improve the efficiency, and hence the profitability, of your company. Through a staff appraisal system you can focus on an individual's efforts within the company, in the context of your business's overall objectives. However in a good scheme it is not just the company which gains from appraisals but ɔ the employees. For instance, employees should:

- Receive recognition for jobs well done.
- Have the chance to discuss problems with you and plan how to solve them.
- Have the opportunity to plan the future development of their job.
- Be able to plan future training with you.
- Know where they stand.

Here are some of the objectives you might wish to achieve for your business:

- Motivation of your staff.
- Assessment of their abilities.
- Improved relationships with your employees.
- Improved communications with your staff.
- Reduction of staff turnover.
- A chance to solve problems relating to job performance.
- An opportunity to identify promotable employees.

Clearly any one appraisal cannot hope to achieve all this – but t. ͟ list should help you to concentrate your mind in deciding what you most wish to achieve from an appraisal scheme.

If you don't have any clear objectives for your appraisal scheme, the best advice is not to bother! Appraisals are not right for every company and yours may well be one of them. A weak appraisal scheme is far worse than not having one at all – your staff will find it frustrating and you will have wasted your time.

Appraisals are not an end in themselves. The best appraisals look towards the future in a positive way. They are sessions in which both you and your employee discuss how these plans can be achieved. Too much criticism of the past will hinder this. Weaknesses must be approached positively – how can they become strengths? Don't let an appraisal interview degenerate into a disciplinary interview. Disciplinary problems must always be treated immediately – don't save up problems just to discuss at appraisal time!

Another thing appraisals should not be about is money! There is no quicker way to lose the objectivity of the exercise than to use it to justify a salary review. Employees will take any criticism as an excuse not to give a bigger pay rise! Arguments could well follow.

ployee's personnel file and job description. Note the key tasks of the job and collect evidence as to how well the job is being performed.

Open the interview by putting the employee at ease and encourage him to talk, explaining that you will be taking notes. As with recruitment interviewing, ask plenty of open questions (How? Why? What? Where? When? Who?) but in addition ask closed questions (requiring only 'yes' or 'no' answers) when you are trying to get to a direct point.

Open up the interview into a two way discussion, and at all costs avoid it becoming a 'tell' session by you. Try to start and end on positive aspects of performance – it will make any criticism more acceptable. Ensure that you cover all the ground needed to complete an appraisal form which gives a true picture of an employee's performance.

Listen actively to what you are being told, maintaining eye contact and giving verbal encouragement. It often helps to summarize what the employee has been saying – to check your understanding and to let him know that you have been listening intently. Explore and expand upon the points he raises – especially his ideas on how to improve performance.

Where there are problems, discuss them frankly – but not as if it were a disciplinary interview. Establish whether or not it is the employee's fault that things are going awry. There may be external constraints causing difficulty. The employee could have some good ideas on how to overcome the problem.

Concentrate on problems which can be solved – not those which can't! For instance, criticisms of personality cannot be constructive.

Agree what can be done to solve a problem. Where appropriate set targets and review dates. Discuss the training required to achieve the objectives.

Encourage the employee to give his opinions on what you are saying. He may well come up with some surprises and also some justified criticism of you! If so, take this in the constructive way in which you expect him to take your criticism!

Here are some 'do's and don'ts' on conducting appraisals:

Do
- Base all your opinions upon fact.
- Be honest with your appraisees.
- Be consistent in your appraisals.
- Be aware of what the employee needs from the appraisal.

Don't
- Raise your employee's expectations too high.

- Base your judgement on limited information. Get as much evidence as you can to back up your judgement – especially if critical.
- Bring your prejudices to the interview.
- Let the 'halo' effect influence you. If the appraisee is excellent in one area there may still be weaknesses in other areas – and vice versa!
- Rate all staff at the extremes of the rating scales, or all safely in the middle.

QUESTIONS AND ANSWERS

How do staff react to appraisals?

It depends how well they are carried out. Poor appraisals are infinitely more damaging than if you had not bothered at all.

Appraisals done well are extremely motivating. Employees are pleased that you have noticed what they are doing, that you appreciate them, that you are listening to their suggestions and generally taking them seriously.

How can wages reflect appraisal assessment?

Paying more to staff who perform better is motivating. It can be infuriating for the hard workers if less committed members of staff earn as much as they do. However for the reasons given above do not link pay increases directly to appraisal.

If your pay rises are given a few months after appraisals a greater or lesser increase can be given, and explained without it affecting the effectiveness of your appraisals in the future.

HOW TO DEVELOP YOUR STAFF

The value of training is not recognised sufficiently in Britain. It should be regarded as an **investment** which will help you to get a good return from all the money you pay out in wages.

The trouble with training is that only rarely can quick and obvious results be seen in cash terms. Once training is over how can you measure what costly errors have been thus avoided? However, over a long period of time you *will* find that the right training helps the bottom line.

It is important to recognise that not *all* problems are training problems. Often sending someone off on a course seems easier than facing up to a problem which has nothing to do with training. When the employee returns from the course, and the problem still exists, poor training is blamed!

If you have problems of recruitment, retaining staff, low standards of work, and if you are plagued by costly errors, training could provide the answer. However, it is important that you follow a planned training programme rather than book the odd course in response to a crisis.

When planning a training programme you need to consider it on three levels. Firstly identify the needs of the company, bearing in mind your mid-to-long term goals. What skills will you require? Which of your staff would be the best training investments? What are your priorities?

As well as considering training on a company level look at the work groups. Could training improve the flexibility of the team? Can they cover for each other during sickness and holidays?

Individual training needs must also be covered and should be identified during appraisals.

Unfortunately training is expensive, both in tuition and in working time 'lost'. Careful planning will help you to get good value for your money. Make sure that you have a very clear objective for each training course you arrange.

If you have staff whom you particularly wish to develop, encourage them to take professional qualifications. You can sponsor them through evening classes, or day release if practical. Local colleges usually provide the best value in training since they are heavily subsidised.

External courses are certainly the easiest to administer, but in some cases on-the-job training can be more practical – especially if there is a simple routine task to impart. In that case identify a suitable **trainer** amongst your staff (or do it yourself) and move through the simple stages of explaining, demonstrating and letting them have a go.

After a course encourage staff fully in the implementation of what they have learned and support them if other staff resent their new ideas. Also get feedback from your employees about the courses so that if you have made a mistake in your choice you don't make it twice. Find out whether:

- The course was well presented.
- It covered the material expected.
- The material was easy to transfer to the workplace.

A course's final assessment cannot be made until the employee has had a chance to put the theory into practice, so assess courses three and six months later, too, to establish the lasting impact.

HOW TO KEEP YOUR STAFF

Why is a high turnover of staff so disastrous? Well, here are just a few reasons:

- Customers won't like speaking to someone different every time they ring.
- It won't enhance the reputation of your company.
- There is the risk of company secrets being lost.
- The hassle and expense of recruitment has to be faced all over again.
- Who will do the work in the interim? You? Someone you are paying to do something else?
- There will now be no return on your training expenses – and the costs will have to be faced again for the new starter.
- The length of time before the new starter is fully competent.

Turnover is established by the following formula:

Number of employees who left during the year x 100
(Average number employed during the year)

So if you have 25 staff and 2 leavers your staff turnover is:

$$\frac{2 \times 100}{25} = 8\%$$

However if your company is very small don't take this formula too seriously! If you have a single member of staff and she decides to leave one year, your staff turnover will be 100%. But this will be less of a problem to you than it would to a multinational!

If you feel that your turnover is too high take a good hard look at the reasons people gave for leaving. Does one keep recurring? Here are some areas which could be the root of your problems:

- Poor recruitment selection.
- Expectations raised too high at interview – disillusionment follows.
- Poor company communications. Employees don't know what they are trying to achieve or why.
- Lack of support from you.
- Low wages.
- Poor working conditions.
- Lack of prospects or new challenges.

CHECKLIST

Appraisals

- Are you sure what you are trying to achieve by having an appraisal scheme?

- Are you going to assess *all* your staff – or just the key employees?

- Have you designed a suitable appraisal form to use?

- Before the interview –

  Have you prepared?
  Have you allowed enough time?
  Have you ensured that there will be no interruptions?

- During the interview –

  Is the employee talking freely?
  Are you listening?
  Are you both agreeing the action to be taken?

- After the interview –
  Does the form accurately reflect what was said?
  Has the employee had a chance to add his comments?
  Have you kept your promises?

Training

- Can you identify the major areas in which training is needed –

  On a company level?
  On a group level?
  On an individual level?

- What skill shortages will you have in the foreseeable future?

Turnover

- Is staff turnover one of your problems?

- Can you identify the root cause?

- The best action to take?

9
Coping with Difficult Employees

Serious problems with your staff will arise only rarely, but the circumstances of each case will be unique – human nature being what it is! However, there are some problems which do arise fairly frequently and we will take a look at these first.

WHAT CAN GO WRONG?

Poor attendance is one of the major banes of an employer's life. As with all difficulties which are potentially disciplinary matters, it is best nipped in the bud before it becomes a major problem.

Most absences are due (or claimed to be due) to sickness. In your company rules it is a good idea to require employees to ring as soon as possible to inform you that they will be absent. Make sure that your employees receive a brief interview after each absence – not a disciplinary interview, but one just to establish what was wrong, how the sickness was treated, and to confirm that they are now fit. This shows that you are concerned about genuine illnesses and is often sufficient to discourage malingerers! If you have a company sick pay scheme ensure that it only pays out at your discretion. If someone has a poor record you have every right to insist upon a doctor's certificate for *every* absence before you give company sick pay. (You cannot apply this to statutory sick pay, however.)

If the absence is not sickness, again speak to the employee to find out what the problem is. He or she could well have a very genuine difficulty which requires your understanding: don't jump to conclusions. The same applies to those who are late for work.

Poor workmanship is another potential difficulty. If you obtained satisfactory references for starters before they joined this should not arise often. Poor workmanship can be a problem of attitude, in which case decisive action must be taken early on. However, it could be a training problem – in which case you must establish the best way in which to solve it.

LAYING DOWN THE LAW

Your disciplinary rules and procedures should primarily encourage an improvement in the behaviour which has caused problems. The penalty aspect should be secondary.

A recurring theme throughout this chapter will be the importance of not jumping to conclusions, giving employees a chance to explain their actions, or omissions, being consistent in your treatment of employees and letting the punishment fit the crime – in essence, being fair.

A major step in this direction is laying down a code of disciplinary and appeal procedures which you will follow when handling these matters. This code should be widely available to your staff so that employees will know where they stand, and know that there will be repercussions for misdemeanours!

Your disciplinary rules should explain the standards you expect with regard to timekeeping, absence, health and safety, and the use of company property and facilities. They should define the sort of action which could constitute gross misconduct, but make it clear that the list is not exhaustive. They should stress that sex and race discrimination will not be tolerated, and explain the appeals procedure.

Another reason for sticking to your procedures is that if you don't you could well lose a case if it were brought to an Industrial Tribunal – even if the dismissal would have otherwise been justified.

Most disciplinary codes have these four stages:

- A verbal warning is literally that. But keep a note of the date, incident and employee's explanation in the personnel file.

- A written warning usually follows if no improvement has followed a verbal warning. If the misdemeanour has been too serious for a verbal warning you can give a written warning on the first offence.

- A final warning letter. Again it follows the previous stage if there has been a further offence. You can go straight to a final warning if the offence is serious enough.

- Dismissal. If the previous warnings have had no effect dismissal is often justified. Likewise if the offence, although only the first, constitutes gross misconduct.

If a really serious disciplinary offence has been committed it is important not to rush into a summary dismissal. If tempers are frayed it is often best to send the employee home, suspended on full pay, while you investigate the incident.

In most disciplinary codes warnings elapse after a certain period.

After any breach of discipline certain steps should be followed to ensure the fair treatment of the employee:

- Investigation
  Define the problem.
  Collect the facts by interviewing witnesses and gathering relevant information – *promptly* after the incident.

- The disciplinary interview
  Let the employee be accompanied by a friend or representative if he wishes.
  Give the employee a chance to explain his view of the events.
  Be willing to consider new evidence.
  Adjourn to investigate if necessary.
  Adjourn to consider your decision.

- The decision. You could decide that:
  There is no case to answer, or
  Further investigation is necessary, or
  Disciplinary action is appropriate.

Your employee may feel that, despite your efforts to be fair, the wrong decision has been reached. He should have the right to appeal against the decision, within a certain time limit. Appeals should be handled without delay and preferably by someone senior to the person who made the decision. Clearly in small companies this will not be possible, in which case you will have to be as impartial as you can in reviewing your decision.

In addition to their *Code of Practice 1 – Disciplinary Practice and Procedures in Employment*, ACAS publish an invaluable advisory handbook *Discipline at Work*. It is free and merits a place on every employer's bookshelf.

THE DISCIPLINARY INTERVIEW

No disciplinary action should take place without first holding a disciplinary interview. It would be like condemning a prisoner without a trial!

The disciplinary interview should be formal. Never hold one in anger in the heat of the moment, and never make it a spectator sport. The interview should only be held in the presence of the employee in question, the person he has chosen to accompany him, yourself and perhaps another member of staff to record the interview if it is a potentially difficult one.

As with other interviews, set aside a time when you will not be interrupted. Make sure that you are thoroughly prepared for the interview. Do you have all the facts at your fingertips?

Try to remain calm but firm throughout the interview. Avoid arguing and any threatening behaviour.

In the interview you should include the following stages:

- Make a statement describing what is being alleged.
- Give the employee an opportunity to state his position. Listen.
- Ask open questions to clarify the position. Stick to facts.
- Summarize the position. Try to agree a plan for improvement, if appropriate.
- Adjourn – either for further investigation or to decide what disciplinary action to take.
- Make your decision, bearing in mind the gravity of the misdemeanour, the employee's past disciplinary record, and the employee's explanation.

THE DISCIPLINARY LETTER

Careful thought needs to go into the writing of a disciplinary letter. Such a letter needs to be rather formal, very accurate and sometimes quite detailed. The employee must be left in no doubt how seriously you view his lapse, or what will happen should the lapse recur. Bear in mind that your letter could be used as evidence in an Industrial Tribunal.

A disciplinary letter should include the following points:

- A clear indication that the letter is a warning/final warning letter.

- A statement that it follows a disciplinary interview (as long as that is the case!). When was it? Who was present?

Dear Frank,

Official Warning Letter

I refer to your disciplinary interview of Friday 13th January. Although given the opportunity you decided not to be accompanied.

The interview was held in connection with the events of the previous day, Thursday 12th January. When I visited your office at 2.00 pm I found that the previous day's takings had been left in your top drawer in a cloth bag ready for banking. The drawer was unlocked.

When I questioned you about this incident you told me that you were going to bank the money later that afternoon. However, you admitted that you were fully aware that takings for the previous day had to be banked by 11.00 am. that morning and in the meantime they had to be placed in the safe.

The security of Company funds is one of the most important aspects of your job and in future you must follow the Operations Manual closely in all your cash handling practices. Leaving Company funds in an unlocked desk drawer is totally unacceptable to the Company and you should know better as a cashier of long standing.

In view of the seriousness with which I view this negligence you are being issued with this warning letter and I expect an immediate and sustained improvement from you in this regard.

Any future failure, in act or omission, regarding this or any other serious matter will result in further disciplinary action in the form of a final warning.

You are reminded of your right to appeal against this warning. It should be made in writing, to me, within 48 hours of receipt of the letter.

Please sign the copy of this letter to confirm receipt.

Yours sincerely, etc.

- A statement of the facts of the complaint. What happened? When did it happen? Who was involved?

- A reference to the employee's explanation (if given) – do you accept it to any extent?

- A confirmation of the improvement you require and over what period.

- A statement clarifying what will happen if there is a recurrence.

- A reminder of the right to appeal.

When you give the letter to the employee it is a good idea to ask him or her to sign a copy as confirmation of receipt – not necessarily indicating his agreement with the contents!

Here are a couple of examples of disciplinary letters, one a warning letter and one a final warning letter:

Dear Jean,

Final warning letter

This letter follows the disciplinary interview which you attended on Thursday 8th June. Your shop steward John Bright, and the shift supervisor Kathryn Brown, were also present.

The interview was held for us to consider the incident on Tuesday 6th June when you were playing cards in the canteen from approximately 10.00 pm until 11.00 pm – a time when you should have been at work.

You received an official warning letter on this very topic just two months ago. Your relapse occurring within such a short period is particularly disappointing to us.

You had no defence to offer regarding the current incident.

The company views this offence in a very serious light, as staff working on night shifts have to be trusted to work, to a large extent, on their own motivation. In view of this it has been decided to issue a final warning letter. *continued*

The other members of staff involved in this incident have also been disciplined.

In future you are only to play cards in the canteen during authorised break times.

Any future failure, in act or omission, in this or any other serious regard will result in further disciplinary action in the form of your dismissal.

If you wish to appeal against this letter you may request an interview with Mr. Smith, within 48 hours of receipt of this letter.

Please sign the copy of this letter to confirm receipt.

Yours sincerely, etc.

THE LAST RESORT

Having exhausted your disciplinary procedures, and presumably your patience, the last resort is the dismissal of the employee.

This is never a decision to be taken lightly – but in the case of employees with over two years' service special care must be taken as the employee has the right to take a complaint of **unfair dismissal** to an Industrial Tribunal.

It is always advisable to obtain legal advice before proceeding with a dismissal of an employee of two years' standing or more.

Dismissal is normally **fair** if the employer has followed his own disciplinary procedures, considered the alternatives, been consistent and acted reasonably. Dismissal is often considered to be a 'reasonable' response from an employer if it is due to one of the following:

- A reason connected with the employee's capability to do the job or qualification for it.
- A reason related to the employee's conduct.
- Redundancy.
- A statutory duty or restriction preventing continued employment.
- Another substantial reason.

Summary dismissal

This is also known as instant dismissal. It is a very drastic step and should only be taken in extreme circumstances. For example:

- A refusal to carry out a reasonable and lawful order.
- Dishonesty.

- Assault to the employer.
- Damage to the employer's property.
- Competition with the employer in business or the disclosure of trade secrets or business records.

Wrongful dismissal

This is not the same as unfair dismissal. A wrongful dismissal occurs when the employer dismisses in **breach of contract**. Usually the breach is that the employer has given less than the contractual notice or no notice at all.

Industrial tribunals have no jurisdiction over wrongful dismissals; the employee has to pursue his claim through the county or high court. The employee's remedy is limited to payment up to the contractual entitlement – for example notice payment.

Constructive dismissal

Dismissal usually occurs when the employer terminates the contract. However events may lead an employee to terminate a contract of employment and claim that he has been 'constructively dismissed'.

This can happen when an employee considers that the employer no longer intends to be bound by the contract because a significant term in the contract has been broken. For example, constructive dismissal could be claimed if you change the working pattern from a day shift to a night shift without consulting your staff and gaining their agreement first.

Employees who claim constructive dismissal have to be decisive. If, in the above instance they had worked the night shift for some time, without complaint, before leaving the company they might be regarded as having had accepted the change in their contract. Therefore they could not claim to have been constructively dismissed.

Constructive dismissal is not necessarily unfair.

Frustration of contract

This occurs when an unforeseeable event makes it impossible for the contract to continue – through no fault of the employer or employee. In this case there is neither a resignation nor a dismissal.

Examples of frustration could be conscription, or a change in law which makes it illegal to employ someone. In some cases long term sickness, injury or imprisonment have been considered to have frustrated a contract of employment.

Unfair dismissal

Claims of unfair dismissal can be made by employees who have been continuously employed for 16 or more hours a week for two years or more, (or between 8 and 16 hours a week for five years). However there is no qualifying period at all if employees have been dismissed on account of their being (or not being) members of a trade union.

Further information is available in the Department of Employment's booklet no. 13, *Unfairly Dismissed?*

QUESTIONS AND ANSWERS

One of my employees is unable to do her job since she became pregnant. Can I dismiss her?

Dismissal just because an employee is pregnant is automatically unfair. However, if the employee is actually *unable* to perform her job due to pregnancy the dismissal may be fair if there is no other suitable alternative vacancy.

An employee has been charged with a criminal offence which has nothing to do with work. Can I dismiss him?

This depends very much on the circumstances of the case. It may be possible to delay action until after the trial. The view of other employees must be taken into account especially if he has been charged with a sexual offence. In this case suspension on full pay until after the trial is probably appropriate.

I want to dismiss an employee with a long term illness. What should I do to ensure, as far as I can, that the dismissal is fair?

You must firstly find out what the medical prognosis is in regard to the employee's continued employment. You must obtain written permission from the employee, to consult his doctor. The employee must be made aware that he has the right to see any medical report before it is supplied by his doctor. Furthermore he has the right to request that it is amended, to attach a statement to it, or to deny the employer the right to see it. In this case you may be forced to make the decision on the information which *is* available to you.

If it appears that the employee will be unable to continue in the present job, a suitable alternative should be considered, such as a less demanding job or early retirement. If dismissal is likely, the employee should be consulted before a firm decision is made (in the presence of a union official, if the union is recognised).

WRITTEN REASONS FOR DISMISSAL

Most employees with over 6 months employment (or part-timers with at least five years service working 8 hours or more a week) have the right to written reasons for dismissal – *if they so request*. (Legislation is planned which will increase the qualifying period for this written statement from 6 months to two years.)

Employers must comply with that request within 14 days. The statement may be used as evidence in an Industrial Tribunal so must be prepared with care. Here is an example of such a letter:

Dear Fiona,

You have requested written reasons for your dismissal which I set out below:

1. Failure to carry out instructions. On the 12th December you were instructed by me to display the Christmas merchandise prominently. When I visited the shop a week later it was evident that you had not followed these instructions. You had been made fully aware of the importance of merchandising seasonal goods to take full advantage of the opportunity for high sales figures during this period. You have been warned on previous occasions regarding the importance of following instructions. This was made clear to you in the warning letter of 13th September and the final warning of 6th November.

2. Timekeeping. Having made enquiries I consider that you have been spending insufficient time at your place of work and this is inconsistent with the carrying out of the duties expected of you as manager of the shop. You have received verbal warnings about this in the last few months and you admit that you find it difficult to get up in the morning and that occasionally you have been leaving early.

For the reasons stated here it was decided that you were to be dismissed with one month's pay in lieu of notice. You were informed about the right to appeal.

Yours, etc.

If you require more details on this subject you may find the Department of Employment's booklet no.14 *Rights to notice and reasons for dismissal* helpful.

A POSSIBLE REPERCUSSION?

The prospect of being brought to face an Industrial Tribunal is not a pleasant one. However, to put the threat in proportion, only a tiny percentage of dismissals reach tribunal stage and of those around 70% fail.

Should a dismissed employee believe that he has been unfairly dismissed he has three months, from the effective date of termination, in which to submit the complaint to an **Industrial Tribunal** – unless it was for some reason impractical for the complaint to be made in time.

To submit a complaint the employee must obtain an **IT1 form** from a Jobcentre. A copy of the completed form will be sent on to the employer and to ACAS. A **conciliation officer** from ACAS will contact one or both of the parties to see whether a voluntary settlement can be reached.

The employer will also receive a form called a **notice of appearance** and it is *essential* that it is completed and returned within 14 days of receipt. If not, the employer will lose the right to contest the case.

A **pre-hearing assessment** can be held at the request of the Tribunal or either party. The assessment is held to consider whether or not the case has substance – but at this stage the case cannot be decided or dismissed. If the Tribunal does not consider that the case has a reasonable prospect of success, costs may be awarded against the ex-employee if he persists with his claim.

If settlement is not reached or the application is withdrawn a Tribunal hearing follows.

Each Industrial Tribunal is made up of a legally qualified chairman and two lay members – one representing employer's organizations and one representing employee's organizations.

If the dismissal is found to be unfair there are three possible remedies:

- Reinstatement – to the same job and with the same terms and conditions, as if the dismissal had never taken place.
- Re-employment – to a different job and possibly different terms and conditions.
- Compensation – a basic award, made on calculations similar to those used for redundancy payments, and a compensatory award in relation to the loss suffered by the employee.

If the employer does not comply with the order for re-instatement or re-employment an additional award may be made to the employee.

Legislation is currently in the pipeline which will enable a chairman of an Industrial Tribunal to demand a **deposit** of £150 from one party as a condition of the case proceeding. The deposit will be required where it is believed that a case has little chance of success or is merely frivolous, vexatious or unreasonable.

CHECKLIST

Disciplinary rules and procedures

- Have you stated your disciplinary rules and procedures in writing?
- Are they freely available to all staff?
- Do they allow for a system of warnings leading to dismissal?
- Is there an appeals procedure?

Disciplinary action

- Have you investigated the circumstances?
- Have you interviewed witnesses?
- Have you got the relevant documentation?
- Have you held a disciplinary interview?
- Did you give the employee every opportunity to explain his actions?
- Have you made the appeals procedure clear to the employee?

Dismissal

- Have you explored the alternatives?
- Have you been consistent?
- Have you been reasonable?
- Have you obtained legal advice?

10
Cutting Back or Ceasing to Trade

Although going out of business can seem an unsavoury subject, it is only proper that you are aware of your obligations to employees if you become insolvent, make redundancies, or need to sell your business.

BUSINESS FOR SALE – STAFF INCLUDED!

The **Transfer of Undertakings Regulations** were introduced in 1977 to give a business's current employees employment protection when the business, or undertaking, in which they are employed changes hands.

The regulations apply where a business is transferred from one owner to another, whether by sale or the death of an owner. It doesn't matter whether it's the business of a sole owner, partnership, or limited company. The regulations are not however applied to changes of ownership effected by a share transfer.

If you combine with another company, to form a third, the staff are considered to have transferred and are under the protection of the regulations.

The regulations state that all employees of the previous owner are automatically transferred to the new owner of the business on the transfer of the undertaking.

Moreover, the new employers are required to observe all the terms and conditions of employment which applied to the employees of the transferred company, prior to the transfer – with the exception of occupational pensions. The employee's continuity of employment is preserved and it is as though the original contract had been made with the new owner. If the new employer makes a fundamental change in the terms and conditions of employment the employees could claim constructive dismissal.

An employee who is dismissed because of the transfer, before or after the event, can claim unfair dismissal. However, the regulations state that if the reason for the dismissal is economic, technical or organizational this may be a reasonable reason justifying dismissal – so you are strongly advised to obtain professional legal advice if you need to consider dismissing staff.

Where a constructive or unfair dismissal is claimed resulting from a transfer of undertakings the fairness of the dismissal would be tested by a tribunal in the usual way.

If you recognise a trade union, the new owner of the business will have to as well – as long as the business retains an individual identity.

Full **consultation** with your staff regarding the transfer of the business is a very good idea as they will, naturally, be very concerned about their futures. If you recognise a union, consultation with your staff is mandatory.

Fuller details on *Employment Rights on the Transfer of an Undertaking* are given in the Department of Employment's free booklet of that title, number 10 in their series.

REDUNDANCY

If you decide that you need to reduce your workforce you may identify certain jobs as being redundant. On the other hand you may find it necessary to reduce your staffing levels and reorganise the way jobs are divided between your remaining employees.

It is not a redundancy if you immediately appoint a replacement for a job previously carried out by a 'redundant' employee.

Before making staff redundant, explore all the other possibilities.

- Can you wait for the natural wastage of staff?
- Can any staff be retired early?
- Is there alternative employment within your business? Clearly these options are more likely if you have a large number of staff.

If you do offer an employee an alternative job, which he unreasonably refuses, he may lose his entitlement to redundancy pay. It is usual to offer an employee a trial period of four weeks in the new job. If either party finds the move unsatisfactory during this period, the employee will be considered to have been made redundant at the point when the original employment ceased. If the employee continues in the job after the end of the trial period, he or she will be regarded as having accepted the new position.

In your dealings with the staff who are to be made redundant, be sensitive to the traumatic effect it will have on them. For many people redundancy can represent loss of status, income, security, social contact with work fellows and often a loss of confidence, too. Try to help in any way you can. If the employee is willing this help could include arranging career counselling, contacting employment agents, helping them to prepare a CV, finding out where there may be other opportunities.

The effect of redundancies will also be disturbing to your company and the staff you retain. There will be a loss of morale amongst your existing staff and some of the staff you need to retain may try to 'read the writing on the wall' and find other jobs. The restructuring of the company will be disruptive unless handled very well. Make sure that they all know where they stand as the situation develops.

You may also have to cope with a certain amount of bad publicity for your business.

If you are planning to make more than 10 people redundant you are required to inform the Secretary of State for Employment, through the Department of Employment.

The staff you lay off may have the following rights:

- The right to have time off to look for another job or to arrange training.
- The entitlement to redundancy payment.

Time Off

Once you have given notice of dismissal because of redundancy, an employee is entitled to a reasonable amount of **paid time off** to look for another job or make arrangements for training – if they meet one of the following criteria:

- They have been employed by you continuously for two years, working sixteen or more hours per week.
- They have been employed by you continuously for five years, working eight or more hours per week.

Redundancy payments

If employees fulfil the above criteria they will be entitled to redundancy payments. (Service before the age of eighteen does not count in this instance.) In addition they must, of course, have been dismissed by reason of redundancy.

Volunteers for redundancy are entitled to full redundancy payment as long as they fulfil the criteria. In some instances if you fail to provide work for an employee over a certain period he may, on his own initiative, claim a redundancy payment.

Part of the amount you pay (currently 35%) can be claimed back from the Department of Employment's **Redundancy Fund** – as long as you have *less than ten employees*. If you decide to pay the employee more than the statutory payment the extra will not qualify for a rebate. The forms you need to make the claims are available from the **Redundancy Payments Office**. You must make your claim within six months of the date that payment was made to the employee. (Unfortunately legislation is being prepared which will abolish this rebate scheme.)

If your cash-flow problems are so serious that the redundancy payments could jeopardize your business, the Department of Employment will pay your employees directly from the Redundancy Fund. You will, however, be expected to repay them at a later date.

The exact amount payable depends on the age of the employee and the number of years' service – up to a maximum of twenty years. The Department of Employment produces a chart to make calculation of payment easy. The principles are however as follows:

- For each complete year of employment in which the employee was over the age of 18 but under 22 years of age – half a week's pay is due.

- For each complete year of employment in which the employee is between the ages of 22 and 41 – one week's pay is due.

- For each complete year of employment in which the employee is over the age of 41 but below 65 for a man, or 60 for a woman, one and a half week's pay is due.

- If the employee is within twelve months of pensionable age, the payment is reduced by one twelfth for each complete month after the 64th birthday, or 59th birthday in the case of women. Employees over pensionable age are not entitled to any redundancy payment. The discrepancy in entitlements to redundancy payment between men and women, due to different retirement ages, will shortly be redressed. Women will be entitled to redundancy payments up to the same age as men.

A week's pay is up to a certain maximum amount laid down by the Department of Employment. This amount is usually adjusted annually.

Employees are not required to pay **tax** on Statutory Redundancy Payments but you can set these payments against tax as a business expense.

Selection for redundancy

In a small business, problems of selection for redundancy rarely arise. However, if you have, say, ten staff doing similar jobs and you need to reduce the workforce by two and reorganize the work between the remaining eight, how do you decide who should go?

The most usually applied principle, and the one most widely accepted by unions, is **last in, first out** – LIFO for short. You could apply this, or you could ask for volunteers first.

If you don't follow the LIFO principle you may have to defend a claim for 'Unfair Selection for Redundancy' – especially if you recognise a union and have previously made an agreement with them to that effect.

Where there is no agreement with a union, the tribunals tend to base their decisions on the rule of LIFO, with the proviso – 'all other things being equal' – so it is best to obtain legal advice if you intend to depart from the LIFO principle.

In addition to handling disputes about selection for redundancy, Industrial Tribunals hear cases on disagreements relating to redundancy payments and the failure to grant time to look for work or to arrange training.

Consultation

If you recognise a trade union you have a **duty to consult** with them about the redundancies before dismissal can take place. Consultation should begin as early as possible, but at least 30 days before the first dismissal if between 10 and 99 employees are to be made redundant. Large companies laying off a 100 or more staff must commence consultation at least 90 days before redundancies are made.

The period of consultation may run concurrently with the employees' notice period.

INSOLVENCY

Certain provisions aimed at protecting an employee's wages apply once a specific event has made an employer legally insolvent. The specific event might be liquidation, receivership or bankruptcy. Ceasing to trade does not itself mean insolvency.

When an employer becomes insolvent his employees receive **preferential** treatment as creditors. Certain arrears in wages and accrued holiday pay are to be settled in full on the termination of the employment. Unlike other payments, there is no qualifying period which has to be served before employee can make a claim under the insolvency provisions. Employees may also claim compensation for not receiving statutory notice and they can apply for redundancy payment if eligible.

Employees apply for payment using forms IP1 and IP2 supplied to them by the liquidator. The completed forms should also be returned to the liquidator. A new employment bill proposes that the Department of Employment will pay certain debts of insolvent employers directly to their employees. The Department's rights to recover such debts are likely to be clarified, too.

If you need more information on redundancies or insolvency, the Department of Employment publish the following booklets which may help you:

Procedure for Handling Redundancies, no. 2 in the series.
Employee's Rights on Insolvency of Employer, no, 3 in the series.
Facing Redundancy? – Time Off for Job-hunting or to Arrange Training, no. 6 in the series.
Redundancy Payments, no. 16 in the series.

This chapter brings the main body of the book to a close. By now you should feel equipped to deal with the more usual tasks and problems which will face you as an employer. You have sufficient information to know where to turn when more unusual problems occur. Most importantly, if you have given thought to the checklists which conclude most chapters, you will have already formulated most of the plans and policies which will help you to become a successful employer.

Appendix One
Health & Safety at Work

There is a great deal of legislation on the topic of health and safety covering both the broad obligations of an employer and obligations of specific industries. Unfortunately the law makes very heavy reading but the consequences of not being aware of your responsibilities could be dire!

Your duties as an employer are to ensure 'as far as reasonably practicable' the health, safety and welfare of those in your employment, during the course of their work. This covers all aspects of providing a hazard free working environment and working practices such as providing safe machinery and maintaining it, handling, storing and transporting articles and substances. The place of work must be maintained to a degree of safety with sufficient entrances and exits. In addition, you must provide personnel with information, training and supervision to ensure health and safety at work.

Unfortunately the Health and Safety at Work Act (1974) is littered with the expression 'as far as is reasonably practicable' which is of course highly subjective. However, in essence, it means that if you perceive a very remote risk which would cost a fortune to prevent, you will be considered a reasonable employer if you do not take action. But if a risk is great, whatever the expense, you must take measures to avoid it. The likelihood of the risk has to be measured against the cost, time and trouble necessary to avoid it.

If you employ more than four people, working at any one time, you will have to issue a statement on your policy regarding Health and Safety.

The Health and Safety Executive have never issued a model statement for employers. They realize that most would adopt it without giving the circumstances of their own business due consideration! Clearly the more hazardous your business the more detailed your statement will have to be.

As a guideline your Health and Safety Policy should include the following:

General policy
Start with a statement saying that you intend to comply with the requirements of the Health and Safety at Work Act (1974) and current legislation, to ensure that the highest standards of safety are practised, at all times, throughout the company.

State your responsibility as an employer, but emphasize that the employees also have a duty to take reasonable care for the health and safety of themselves and others who may be affected by their acts and omissions at work. Employees must also cooperate to comply with the statutory requirements laid down.

Organization
Make it clear how, and to whom, employees are to report matters regarding health and safety at work.

If you have a safety advisor, or perhaps a safety representative or committee, their function must be described.

If you recognise a union they have a right to appoint safety representatives from the workforce. If two or more of these representatives request that a safety committee is formed you have a statutory duty to comply.

Arrangements for carrying out the policy
The major cause of accidents is the employees' lack of awareness of the hazards involved in their work. So the identification of potential dangers is important in this section of your policy, along with the details of precautions to be taken. These could include the use of protective clothing, working practices and the use of machinery and maintenance procedures.

The compilation of your policy gives you a good opportunity to consider the possible hazards of your business but remember to review them regularly and amend the policy when appropriate.

The Health and Safety at Work Act is administered by the **Health and Safety Commission** whose role is to research and give advice. The **Health and Safety Executive** is the operational and enforcing arm and is responsible for the **Health and Safety Inspectorate**. Health and

Safety Inspectors have very far-ranging powers should they suspect a dangerous situation on your premises.

If an inspector finds that you are in breach of the relevant statutory provisions he may issue you with either:

- An **improvement notice** which states that the breach must be remedied within a specified period. Or
- A **prohibition notice** demanding that activities, which he has identified as causing serious risk of injury, stop immediately.

There are Inspectorate addresses throughout the country and one of the head offices will be able to put you in touch with the right one:

Health and Safety Inspectorate
Baynards House
1 Chepstow Place
London W2 4TF
(01) 229-3456

Health and Safety Inspectorate
Magdalen House
Trinity Road
Merseyside L20 3QZ
(051) 951-4000

You have a legal obligation to report any:

- Fatal accidents
- Major injury accidents/conditions
- Dangerous occurrences
- Accidents causing more than three days incapacity for work
- Certain work-related diseases
- Certain matters dealing with the safe supply of gas.

Further details are available from the Health and Safety Inspectorate.

Keep records of all accidents in an **accident book**. This must be kept on the premises and be available for inspection for at least three years after the accident.

Record:

- The date and time of the accident
- The name of the injured person and details of the injury
- The place where the accident happened
- A brief description of the circumstances.

Reportable diseases are those which are work-related. They include certain cases of poisoning, skin diseases, lung diseases, infections and other conditions. Apply to the Health and Safety offices for full details.

In the case of a reportable disease record:

- The date of diagnosis
- The name and occupation of the person affected
- The name and nature of the disease.

There are many regulations regarding specific industries or places of work (Factories, Shops, Offices, etc) and the Health and Safety Inspectorate will be able to advise you which, if any, apply to your business. They will also be able to supply Health and Safety booklets for your guidance.

This appendix is only an introduction to health and safety at work. As it is so important to be fully aware of the regulations relating to your business, a copy of the *Health and Safety at Work Act* is an essential item for your bookshelf. It is available from HMSO. Although the Health and Safety Regulations seem daunting, do remember that they are there to prevent accidents – not to catch you out! So if you need help ask for official guidance.

First Aid

Every employer must have at least one **First Aid Box**. It must be clearly identified (ideally green with a white cross on it) and suitable for the purpose. It should keep the contents free from damp and dust. Some employees may need travelling first-aid kits.

The contents of the box should be as follows:

Item	*Number of employees*		
	1-5	6-10	11-50
First-aid guidance card	1	1	1
Individually wrapped sterile adhesive dressings	10	20	40
Sterile eye pads with attachment	1	2	4
Triangular bandages	1	2	4
Safety pins	6	6	12
Sterile unmedicated dressings			
Medium	3	6	8
Large	1	2	4
Extra large	1	2	4

More supplies are required if you have over 50 staff.

If you have fewer than 150 staff and are working in a low hazard business it is only necessary to have an 'Appointed Person' to deal with first aid. If there are serious hazards in your business, or you have over 150 staff, one or more of your staff must be trained and qualified in first aid. Recognised courses are run by the St. John Ambulance Brigade amongst others. You must inform your employees of the arrangements you have made for first aid and all first aid treatments must be recorded – you could use the Accident Book (see above).

Full details regarding first aid requirements are available from HMSO. Ask for *The Approved Code of Practice* and *The Guidance Notes* which have been prepared by the Health and Safety Executive.

Fire precautions

Make sure that all employees know what to do in case of fire – this may include training in the use of fire extinguishers, locations of fire exits, fire drills – depending on the size and nature of your business.

Fire safety is supervised by the **Fire Authority** who control the issue of **Fire Certificates**. These are required by most businesses but some small businesses may be exempt. Full details of exemptions and the regulations with which you must comply are available from the Health and Safety Executive.

Appendix Two
The Law and You

This section lists, alphabetically, the major laws likely to affect you as an employer. Just a brief outline of some of the major points in the acts relating to employment are given. This section does not pretend to give a definitive statement of the law.

The Acts themselves are available from Her Majesty's Stationery Office.

It is essential to keep up to date in matters of law – things can change very rapidly. A good solution to the problem is to subscribe to an updating service. An excellent example is *Croner's Reference Book for Employers*. This is a loose leaf book and subscribers receive up to date information on a monthly basis. This is available from Croner Publications Limited, Croner House, London Road, Kingston-upon-Thames, Surrey KT2 6SR, (01) 547 3333.

ACCESS TO MEDICAL REPORTS ACT 1988

Individuals have the right of access to any medical report relating to them, supplied by their doctor for employment or insurance purposes. Under this act employees may also refuse you access to these records.

This means that before requesting a medical report from an employee's doctor, the employer must notify the employee, in writing, that the doctor is to be approached, the employee must also be notified of his or her rights. Consent from the employee must be obtained, also in writing, prior to consulting the doctor.

The employee's rights are as follows:

- The right to withhold consent for the employer to consult his or her doctor.

- The right to state that he or she wishes to see the report before it is given to the employer.
- The right to request that the report is amended.
- The right to attach a statement to the report.
- The right to refuse the employer access to the report, after the employee has seen it.
- The right to request access to the report, via the doctor, at any time up to six months after it was requested.

ATTACHMENT OF EARNINGS ACT 1971

This Act applies only to England and Wales. It comes into effect when a person has **defaulted on a court order** to pay a debt, fine, or maintenance, by means of regular payments. The courts may make an attachment order for the person's employer to make the deductions and forward them to the court.

CHILDREN AND YOUNG PERSONS ACT 1933 – 1969

Those under the school leaving age are 'children' under this Act. The Act states that no child under 13 may be employed; the periods and times which children over the age of 13 are allowed to work are regulated.

CONTROL OF SUBSTANCES HAZARDOUS TO HEALTH REGULATIONS 1988

This is the most far reaching Health and Safety legislation since the Health and Safety at Work Act 1974. The regulations come into effect on October 1st, 1989. The regulations aim to control the exposure of employees to hazardous substances whilst at work.

Employers must ensure that suitable and sufficient assessments are made of every hazardous substance used or generated in the workplace. When a risk of exposure has been identified the exposure must be eliminated or, if this is not possible, adequately controlled. Employees who are exposed must be subject to monitoring and health surveillance.

Employers are obliged to instruct, inform and train all employees who may be exposed to hazardous substances during the course of their work. All employers are strongly advised to obtain full information from the Health and Safety Executive.

DATA PROTECTION ACT 1984

This Act was introduced to regulate the use of data, relating to individuals if held in a form which can be accessed by computer. This includes employees and so if you computerise your personnel records you will have to register.

DEFAMATION ACT 1952

When a reference is given, information regarding a person's character is given. If this is untrue and is designed to damage the person he or she may make a claim for damages.

DISABLED PERSONS (EMPLOYMENT) ACT 1944 AND 1958

This Act is designed to help disabled people to obtain employment or set up in business themselves. Companies with 20 or more staff are required to employ a quota of disabled people. This quota is currently 3%.

EDUCATION (WORK EXPERIENCE) ACT 1973

Regulations prohibiting the employment of children do not apply to periods of 'work experience' if it is part of the child's education and is approved by the local education authority.

EMPLOYMENT ACT 1988

This Act is unlikely to affect employers of small numbers of staff as it is mainly concerned with the rights of trade union members. The main provisions of this Act are that:
- Union members are granted the right not to be instructed to take part in industrial action without the support of a ballot.
- Union members have the right not to be unjustifiably disciplined if they refuse to participate in industrial action.
- The closed shop no longer has legal protection.
- In some circumstances separate ballots on industrial action must be held in the different workplaces.
- Union members may elect trade union leaders by secret postal ballot.
- A commissioner for the rights of trade union members has been appointed.

THE EMPLOYMENT BILL

Late in 1988 the draft of a proposed new Act of Parliament was released. At the time of writing it is believed that this legislation is to be introduced as soon as parliamentary time permits. The major provisions are as follows:

- Legislation which discriminates between men and women in employment and training will be repealed. However, in special circumstances, where the health of an unborn child could be at risk protection for women will be retained.
- Restrictions upon the hours of work for young people will be removed – including night work. Other restrictions concerning the employment of young people will also be lifted – but not those controlling work with dangerous machinery or substances.
- Women will be entitled to statutory redundancy payments up to the same age as men.
- The scheme where employers with fewer than 10 employees may claim rebates on statutory redundancy payments is to be abolished.
- The Training Commission will be dissolved.
- Those employing fewer than 20 will be exempted from providing particulars of any disciplinary procedures which may apply to the employees.
- The amount of time allowed off, with pay, for lay trade union officials on trade union duties or training, will be limited.
- The qualifying period for a written statement of the reasons for dismissal will be extended from 6 months to two years.
- A chairman of an Industrial Tribunal may require a deposit of £150 from one party as a condition of proceeding further with the case. This may occur when it is considered that the case has little prospect of success, or that pursuing the case would be frivolous, vexatious or unreasonable.
- The Department of Employment will pay certain debts of insolvent employers to their employees. The department's rights to recover such debts will be clarified.

EMPLOYMENT OF CHILDREN ACT 1973

Until this Act comes into force, permits to employ children must be obtained from the local education authority.

EMPLOYMENT PROTECTION (CONSOLIDATION) ACT 1978

As amended in 1980 and 1982

This Act consolidates legislation on the individual rights of employees. The major provisions are:

- **Written particulars** of terms of employment for all employees, working 16 or more hours per week, within 13 weeks of starting. See the Department of Employment's Employment Legislation leaflet number 1 – one of a series of leaflets available from the Jobcentre.

- The requirement to provide staff with **itemised pay statements**. See Employment Legislation leaflet number 8.

- **Guarantee payments**. In certain circumstances these are to be made to employees if you are unable to supply work for them to do. Failure to pay can be remedied through an Industrial Tribunal. See Employment Legislation leaflet number 9.

- **Medical suspension**. Many employees, suspended from work on medical grounds, in compliance with statutory provisions or a code of practice issued under the Health and Safety at Work Act, are entitled to payment. This does not include employees who are medically unfit for work. See Employment Legislation leaflet number 5.

- Covers the right to belong, or not to belong, to a trade union. See Employment Legislation leaflet number 7.

- **Time Off Work**. Employees have the right to paid time off for trade union duties (officials) or activities. See the ACAS Code of Practice Number 3. The right to unpaid leave exists for those with public duties such as justices of the peace and school governors. See Employment Legislation leaflet number 12. Several employees under notice of redundancy have the right to a reasonable amount of time off with pay for job hunting or to make arrangements for training. See Employment Legislation leaflet number 6. Paid time off must also be given for ante-natal care. See Employment Legislation leaflet number 4.

- **Breach of Contract**. Dismissal without notice or without notice payment could be a breach of contract. Damages could be payable through a county court. Likewise an employer is entitled to claim damages from an employee who leaves without giving proper notice – but this is rarely done.

- **Maternity rights**. Statutory maternity pay and the right to return. This is also covered by Employment Legislation leaflet number 4.

- **Summary Dismissal.**

- **Entitlement to written reasons for dismissal**. See Employment Legislation leaflet number 14.

- **The right not to be unfairly dismissed**. See Employment Legislation leaflet number 13.

- The right to **Redundancy Payments**. See Employment Legislation leaflet number 16.

- **The insolvency of the employer**. See Employment Legislation leaflet number 3. If the business is to be transferred see also leaflet number 10.

- **Industrial Tribunals** – jurisdiction and remedies.

EQUAL PAY ACT 1970

Under this Act men and women, working full or part-time, are entitled to equal treatment in their terms and conditions of employment in instances where they are employed to do the same or similar work, or alternatively work of equal value.

FACTORIES ACT 1961

This Act lays out several matters relating to factories. It is gradually being replaced by regulations and codes of practice. It covers premises, working conditions and various aspects of safety.

FIRE PRECAUTIONS ACT 1971

Covers fire safety in all places of work.

HEALTH AND SAFETY AT WORK ACT 1974

This warrants a section on its own! See Appendix One.

MISREPRESENTATION ACT 1967

If a person enters into a contract, including a contract of employment, and suffers damage due to the misrepresentation of terms, a claim for damages may be made.

OCCUPIERS' LIABILITY ACT 1984

Under this Act occupiers of a premises have the duty to take reasonable care for the safety of people, other than visitors, in defined cases where there is a risk of danger. The occupier's duty is discharged by warning people and discouraging them to take the risk.

OFFICES, SHOPS AND RAILWAY PREMISES ACT 1963

This is largely superseded by the Health and Safety at Work Act 1974 but several provisions still apply. It covers working conditions and aspects of safety.

RACE RELATIONS ACT 1976

No employer, regardless of the numbers they employ, may discriminate on racial grounds. Employers are also liable for an employee's discrimination if it occurs at work.

In the recruitment of staff, you must not discriminate in your selection procedures. This includes the use of unreasonable selection tests, which could constitute indirect discrimination.

The failure to offer a job, on grounds of race, would clearly be racial discrimination. Existing employees must not be discriminated against in their terms of their employment, promotion, training or any other benefit. Nor may you dismiss, or impose any other penalty on racial grounds.

It is worth obtaining the Code of Practice from the **Commission for Racial Equality**.

REHABILITATION OF OFFENDERS ACT 1974

With exceptions, a person with a conviction may treat it as if it never happened, if after a period of rehabilitation, no further serious offence has been committed. The conviction then becomes 'spent'.

An employer may ask a job applicant whether he has a conviction but the candidate is not obliged to admit to a spent conviction. Employers may not ask if the applicant has a spent conviction.

It is unlawful for an employer to discriminate against an employee with a spent conviction. Nor may the employee be dismissed for that reason.

The period of rehabilitation before a conviction becomes spent varies with the length of the sentence. Sentences of over two and a half years do not become spent.

SEX DISCRIMINATION ACTS 1975 AND 1986

It is unlawful to discriminate on the grounds of sex, in the recruitment of staff, the terms of full or part-time employment, in training or promotion.

Discrimination against a woman occurs where, on the grounds of her sex, she is treated less favourably than a man. Both direct and indirect discrimination are unlawful.

The Act protects men as well as women.

You may not discriminate against people on the grounds of their marital status.

The Code of Practice would be a useful addition to your bookcase – copies may be obtained from the Equal Opportunities Commission.

SHOPS ACTS 1950 AND 1965

These Acts were introduced to ensure that the hours worked by shop assistants were not excessive and that they had sufficient breaks during the working day. A copy is essential for all employers in the retail trade.

TRADE UNION AND LABOUR RELATIONS ACT 1974 AND 1976

As amended by the Employment Acts of 1980 and 1982 and the Trade Union Act 1984

These acts legislate on several topics including: 'no-strike' clauses, trade disputes, lawful secondary action, picketing, ballots, union dues and employee involvement. Codes of Practice concerning these acts are available from ACAS.

UNFAIR CONTRACT TERMS 1977

An employer cannot restrict his liability for death or personal injury, resulting from negligence, by means of a term in a contract.

WAGES ACT 1986

This repeals the Truck Acts and as a result manual workers no longer have the statutory right to be paid in the coin of the realm. However changing this term of employment for your current workforce could, conceivably, result in a claim of 'constructive dismissal'. Deductions from pay are also governed by this Act.

YOUNG PERSONS (EMPLOYMENT) ACTS 1938 AND 1963

This regulates the hours of work for young people working in certain businesses. A 'young person' is one over school-leaving age but under eighteen.

Glossary

Absenteeism A term used to describe levels of absence due to illness or malingering. Often expressed in terms of a percentage, the average level of absenteeism in Britain currently runs at 7% – which is far too high!

ACAS This stands for Advisory, Conciliation and Arbitration Service. ACAS plays an important role in advising and supplying information on industrial relations to employers. Its officers play a conciliatory role in trying to solve trade disputes and complaints made to Industrial Tribunals.

Appraisal An assessment of an employee's current performance with a view to the future – problem solving, training, development, or identifying promotion potential.

Assertiveness How to get your own way a little more often – charmingly – whilst never losing sight of other people's rights or your own.

Casual workers The term refers to staff who are employed for a period of a week or less – not to lazy employees!

Closed shop Where union membership is a condition of employment. Also known as Union Membership agreements.

Constructive dismissal This occurs when the employer does something to break the employment contract. Examples include reducing rates of pay and changing hours of work or the place of work, without the employee's consent. Constructive dismissal can also occur if an employer's behaviour is unbearable or the employee is given the choice of resigning or being dismissed. If an employee is found to be constructively dismissed he may claim unfair dismissal. However, a constructive dismissal may well be a fair dismissal.

Communications Most companies put too little emphasis on 'good communications'. Companies in which rumour and the grapevine abound should look carefully at ways of opening up good communications channels so that the right information can flow freely between staff, upwards and downwards.

Counselling Don't worry too much about lack of expertise in this. The art of good counselling is listening, and asking questions which will lead the employee to reach his or her *own* conclusions.

Contracts of employment In practice most employees are given a short 'statement of main terms and conditions' instead. This is quite adequate. All employees should receive a statement, or contract, within 13 weeks of starting work.

Data protection Not the protection of *your* computer data but the individual's rights concerning the information you hold about them. Computer users, including employers, who hold personal data must register under the Data Protection Act.

Delegation One of the keys to successful management – letting your employees do some of the work!

Disciplinary code A set of rules which will let your employees know what standards of discipline you expect – and what will happen if these standards are not met.

DSS Department of Social Security (formerly DHSS, Department of Health and Social Security).

ET Employment Training – YTS for grown-ups.

Employment legislation The term used for the ever increasing number of laws relating to employment. The major laws are described in Appendix Two, but always be on the lookout for new developments and amendments.

Industrial Tribunal. Quasi-judicial body for resolving disputes on employment issues.

Interview 'Inter' means between. The interview should be a mutual discussion between two parties meeting with a 'view' to establishing whether they could possibly work together.

Motivation The carrot rather than the stick.

Reprimand An unpleasant session with an errant employee which usually leaves *you* feeling more depressed than the employee.

Service contract Term usually applied to longer employment contracts drawn up by solicitors for senior staff.

Statutory Required by Act of Parliament or legislation.

Summary dismissal Instant dismissal – only to be used in extreme circumstances.

Time management How to put *the* most valuable resource to the best use.

Unfair dismissal A dismissal which was not a 'reasonable' response by the employer in the circumstances.

Wrongful dismissal In which you are in breach of the contract – usually in failing to make a notice payment.

YTS The much maligned Youth Training Scheme, which has in fact proved beneficial to the majority of trainees and employers alike.

Further Reading

General
Assertiveness at Work, David Stubbs (Pan Books 1985).
Croner's Guide to Absence (Croner Publications 1986).
Effective Management Skills, John Scott and Arthur Rochester (Sphere Books and the British Institute of Management 1984).
Employing People (ACAS 1987).
Improve Your People Skills, Peter Honey (Institute of Personnel Management 1988).
The One Minute Manager, Kenneth Blanchard and Spencer Johnson (Fontana 1982).
Recruitment and Selection, Philip Plumbley (Institute of Personnel Management 1968).
So You Think You Can Manage? Video Arts (Methuen 1984).
Success in Management: Personnel, Penny Hackett (John Murray, revised 1987).
The Time Trap, R. Alec Mackenzie (McGraw-Hill 1972).
Training Interventions, John Kenney and Margaret Reid (Institute of Personnel Management 1986).

Free ACAS booklets
Employing People: The ACAS Handbook for Small Firms.
Discipline at Work: The ACAS Advisory Handbook.
Advisory Booklets Series:
    No.1. – Job Evaluation.
    No.2 – Introduction to Payment Systems.
    No.3 – Personnel Records.
    No.4 – Labour Turnover.
    No.5 – Absence.
    No.6 – Recruitment and Selection.
    No.7 – Induction of New Employees.

No.8 – Workplace Communications.
No.9 – The Company Handbook.
No.10 – Employment Policies.

Free booklets from the Department of Employment
The following are published in the Employment Legislation Series:
No.1 – Written statement of main terms and conditions of employment.
No.2 – Procedure for handling redundancies.
No.3 – Employee's rights on insolvency of employer.
No.4 – Employment rights for the expectant mother.
No.5 – Suspension on medical grounds under health and safety regulations.
No.6 – Facing redundancy? Time off for job hunting or to arrange training.
No.7 – Union membership rights and the closed shop.
No.8 – Itemized pay statements.
No.9 – Guarantee payments.
No.10 – Employment rights on the transfer of an undertaking.
No.11 – Rules governing continuous employment and a week's pay.
No.12 – Time off for public duties.
No.13 – Unfairly dismissed?
No.14 – Rights to notice and reasons for dismissal.
No.15 – Union secret ballots.
No.16 – Redundancy payments.

Employment law
There are several publications which will keep you up to date on developments in Employment Law. One of the best ways is to subscribe to a loose leaf manual which is updated regularly.

Reference Book for Employers (Croner Publications).
Janner's Employment Letters, Greville Janner (Business & Legal Publications).
The Encyclopaedia of Employment Law and Practice, Frank Walton (Professional Publishing).
Employment Law (Croner Publications).

Alternatively you can subscribe to a magazine. Among the best are:
Employment Digest (Croner Publications).
Industrial Relations Legal Information Bulletin (Industrial Relations Service, London).

Useful Addresses

Advisory, Conciliation and Arbitration Service (ACAS)
27 Wilton Street
London SW1X 2AZ
Tel: (01) 210 3600

Commission for Racial Equality
Elliot House
10/12 Allington Street
London SW1E 5EH
Tel: (01) 828 7022

Data Protection Registrar
Springfield House
Water Lane
Wilmslow
Cheshire SK9 5AX
Tel: (0625) 53 5777

Department of Employment
Caxton House
Tothill Street
London SW1H 9NF
Tel: (01) 213 3000

Equal Opportunities Commission
Overseas House
Quay Street
Manchester M3 3HN
Tel: (061) 833 9244

Health and Safety Inspectorate
Baynards House
1 Chepstow House
1 Chepstow Place
London W2 4TF
Tel: (01) 229 3456

Health and Safety Inspectorate
Magdalen House
Trinity Road
Bootle
Merseyside L20 3QZ
Tel: (051) 951 4000

Her Majesty's Stationery Office (HMSO)
49 High Holborn
London WC1V 6HB
Tel: (01) 622 3316

Training Agency
Moorfoot
Sheffield S1 4PQ
Tel: (0742) 753275

Wages Council Office
Steel House
11 Tothill Street
London SW1H 9NF
Tel: (01) 213 3881

Index

127